Valiantly Forging Ahead!!

CRO MAR TIE HIGH

1 EIJI NONAKA

HISTORY OF TOKYO METROPOLITAN CROMARTIE HIGH SCHOOL

1923   Establishment of Tokyo Prefectural 49th Junior High School. Tokyo Prefectural Teacher College Vice Principal, Shigenoshin Mizuhara, is named Principal. The school building is completely destroyed in the Great Kanto Earthquake that same year.

1930   Tetsuharu Kawakami assumes office as the first Kingpin-General. Is famous for having said, "The guy was moving so slow I didn't know he was actually fighting."

1943   Following the establishment of the Tokyo Metropolitan Government, the school name is changed to Tokyo Metropolitan 49th Junior High School.

1944   The 1st Battle of the Strongest Street Fighter Competition is held. Due to air raids, a winner is unable to be determined.

1945   End of World War II

1948   School is reclassified as Tokyo Metropolitan 49th High School under the new educational system.

1950   Name of school is changed to Tokyo Metropolitan Cromartie High School under Regulation Number 1 set forth by the Tokyo Metropolitan Board of Education.

1951   Creation of Cromartie High School Parent-Teacher Association.

1952   Inauguration Ceremony held after completion of the new school building.

1956   Inauguration Ceremony held upon successful completion of the gymnasium and swimming pool.

1960   Cromartie High hosts the 1st general assembly for the All-Tokyo Kingpin Association. Kingpin, Shigeo Nagashima, is quoted as saying, "Cromartie High will forever be indestructible."

1968   Police intervention at the graduation ceremony develops into an extraordinary 5-on-5 brawl.

1969   In a sudden and unprecedented turn of events, all students and faculty alike become lost in Kyoto while on a school trip.

1970   The Kingpin Association moves to change its name and convenes, now as the Kingpin Summit.

1975   The Cromartie High baseball club advances to the 2nd round of the summer All-Japan High School Baseball Championships.

1978   The school's first Choral Competition is held. Class 2-3 wins the group competition with their performance of "Yume wa Yoru Hiraku."

1980   The legendary "Mysterious School Building Explosion Incident" occurs. Classes are suspended for two weeks.

1981   Reconstruction of the school building is completed.

1987   In another unprecedented turn of events, the entire faculty and student body forget what day the matriculation ceremony is to be held. New students are left in a state of confusion.

1995   Commencement of the study abroad student exchange program. Relationship with foreign sister school suddenly deteriorates.

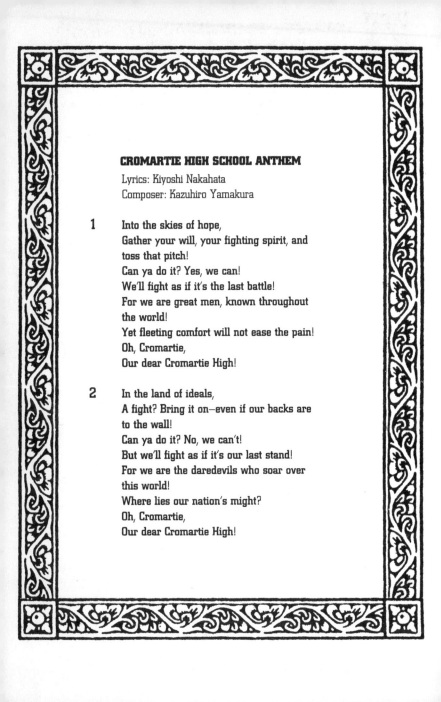

CROMARTIE HIGH SCHOOL ANTHEM

Lyrics: Kiyoshi Nakahata
Composer: Kazuhiro Yamakura

1   Into the skies of hope,
    Gather your will, your fighting spirit, and
    toss that pitch!
    Can ya do it? Yes, we can!
    We'll fight as if it's the last battle!
    For we are great men, known throughout
    the world!
    Yet fleeting comfort will not ease the pain!
    Oh, Cromartie,
    Our dear Cromartie High!

2   In the land of ideals,
    A fight? Bring it on—even if our backs are
    to the wall!
    Can ya do it? No, we can't!
    But we'll fight as if it's our last stand!
    For we are the daredevils who soar over
    this world!
    Where lies our nation's might?
    Oh, Cromartie,
    Our dear Cromartie High!

TABLE OF CONTENTS

DEAR MOTHER, I HAVE MANAGED TO ENROLL AT CROMARTIE HIGH SCHOOL.

TOKYO METRO CROMARTIE HIGH

HOWEVER...

HOPEFULLY, I WILL BE ABLE TO ADJUST TO SCHOOL LIFE HERE AS SOON AS POSSIBLE, AND WITHOUT ISSUE.

TAKASHI KAMIYAMA, 16

I FIND, BEING SURROUNDED BY ALL THESE UNFAMILIAR INDIVIDUALS SOMEWHAT BEWILDERING.

THIS IS ME, RIGHT HERE.

OH, NO!

ACTUALLY, THEY LOOK LIKE A PRETTY **BAD** BUNCH OF GUYS. I'M SO NERVOUS I CAN'T EVEN HOLD MY PENCIL STEADY...

SILLY ME! I GUESS THERE ARE GOOD PEOPLE HERE, TOO.

OH... THANK YOU.

HM?

fwp

WHAT THE--?!

SNAP

HE... **ATE** MY PENCIL. AH, BUT CROMARTIE **IS** FAMOUS FOR ITS DELINQUENT STUDENTS. THIS IS MOST UNUSUAL...

crnch crnch

=GULP=

CLATTER

UMPH

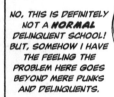

NO, THIS IS DEFINITELY NOT A **NORMAL** DELINQUENT SCHOOL! BUT, SOMEHOW I HAVE THE FEELING THE PROBLEM HERE GOES BEYOND MERE PUNKS AND DELINQUENTS.

gag
BARF

HE... HE ATE THEM!

GRMPH

Y... YEAH.

HEY, KAMIYAMA! YOU BROUGHT THE MONEY, RIGHT?

OH, THAT'S RIGHT! I REMEMBER A COUPLE YEARS AGO, WHEN I WAS IN 7TH GRADE... I USED TO GET BULLIED ALL THE TIME FOR BEING A "PENCILNECK."

HOW DID I EVER END UP IN A PLACE LIKE THIS?

THAT WAS WHEN I FIRST MET ICHIRO YAMAMOTO.

IF IT'S MONEY YA WANT, GO GET A DAMN JOB!

YOU WANT TO GET HURT?

WHO THE HELL ARE YOU?

KAMIYAMA! WHAT'RE YA DOING GIVIN' THOSE PISSANTS **MONEY?**

IF I HAD JUST GIVEN THEM THE MONEY, THERE WOULDN'T HAVE BEEN ANY PROBLEM...

WHY DID YOU DO THAT? WE'RE NOT EVEN FRIENDS.

OUCH! MAN, I GUESS I CAN'T WIN 3 ON 1...

BUT THAT'S YOUR **PARENTS'** MONEY, RIGHT? YOU AIN'T THE ONE THAT SAVED IT UP, SO DON'T GO ACTIN' ALL BIG!

UNGH!

whap

EVENTUALLY IT CAME TIME FOR THE HIGH SCHOOL ENTRANCE EXAMS...

YAMAMOTO GAVE ME THE COURAGE TO STAND UP TO BULLYING.

I'M SORRY. YOU'RE RIGHT...

WELL, GOING TO HIGH SCHOOL ISN'T NECESSARILY THE MOST IMPORTANT THING IN THE WORLD... BUT WEREN'T YOU TELLING ME YOU WANTED TO CONTINUE STUDYING?

NAH. NO POINT IN **ME** GOIN' TO A PLACE LIKE THAT.

WHAT? YOU'RE NOT GOING ON TO HIGH SCHOOL?

GIMME A DAMN BREAK! WHO THE HECK IS GONNA BE ABLE TO LEARN ANYTHING AT A DUMBASS SCHOOL LIKE THAT?

GO TO **CROMARTIE!** YOU'LL BE ACCEPTED THERE JUST FOR BEING ABLE TO ADD AND SUBTRACT!

THERE AIN'T NO SCHOOLS THAT'LL TAKE STUPID PUNKS LIKE ME, THOUGH.

THE DESIRE TO STUDY IS WHAT'S MOST IMPORTANT! IF YOU HAVE THE **WILL**, YOU CAN LEARN IN ANY ENVIRONMENT... EVEN AT **CROMARTIE.**

PAY-BACK FOR EARLIER.

WHAT THE HELL WAS THAT FOR?

UNGH!

whap

I'M GOING TO PROVE WHAT I SAID BEFORE, THAT YOU CAN STUDY **ANY-WHERE.**

YOU'RE SERIOUS? YOU KNOW YOU COULD GET INTO A MUCH BETTER SCHOOL.

TOKYO METRO CROMARTIE HIGH SCHOOL

ENROLLMENT REGISTRATION

THEN WHY DON'T WE **BOTH** ENROLL THERE?

THAT'S A DAMN LIE! JUST MORE OF YOUR FANCY TALK!

MY FRIENDSHIP WITH YAMAMOTO IS WHAT BROUGHT ME TO THIS SCHOOL.

I'M NOT SURE I COULD DO IT ALONE, BUT **TOGETHER** MAYBE WE CAN MANAGE, MAYBE EVEN CHANGE THINGS...

BUT CROMARTIE'S NOTHING BUT A HANGOUT FOR PUNKS.

HOWEVER, THERE'S JUST ONE THING I HADN'T COUNTED ON...

I HAVE NO REGRETS.

YAMAMOTO WAS UNABLE TO PASS THE ENTRANCE EXAM.

HE WAS **THAT** STUPID?

WHY DID YOU COME HERE?

-10-

OH, YEAH?

MAN, I'VE BEEN BAD SINCE **MIDDLE SCHOOL.**

TODAY'S TOPIC— THE BRAGGING CONTEST: "YEAH, I USED TO BE A BAD BADASS"

OH, YEAH? WELL, I MADE A NAME FOR MYSELF, TOO!

YEP.

YOU'RE THE LEGENDARY "FIREBALL" FROM 2ND MIDDLE SCHOOL?

THEY ALL SAID I WAS OUTTA CONTROL. "THE FIREBALL OF 2ND" WAS WHAT THEY CALLED ME.

THAT DOESN'T SOUND VERY COOL...

"THE HOSPITA-LIZER"?

THAT'S WHY THEY CALLED ME "THE HOSPITA-LIZER OF 3RD."

IF I EVER LOST CONTROL, I WOULDN'T LET UP UNTIL MY OPPONENT WAS A BLOODY PULP.

SEE, I **LOOK** SO DAMN TOUGH THAT NOBODY EVEN TRIED TO START ANYTHING WITH ME.

WHAT THE HELL?!

I WAS PRETTY BAD MYSELF... BUT I NEVER GOT IN A SINGLE FIGHT.

SO IS HE AWESOME, OR DOES HE SUCK? I DON'T GET IT...

DUNNO. I TOLD YOU-- I AIN'T BEEN IN A **SINGLE** FIGHT.

BUT CAN YOU REALLY FIGHT OR WHAT?

SO I GOT THE NICKNAME "MASA, THE CHAMP BY DEFAULT."

I WAS **ALWAYS** GETTING IN FIGHTS. AND I NEVER LOST A SINGLE ONE. WITH ME IT WAS ALWAYS SWING FIRST AND TALK LATER. WHEN IT COMES TO BADASSES, I'M THE REAL DEAL.

HM?

I'LL TELL YA STRAIGHT-- YOU'VE ALL GOT **NOTHING** ON ME!

HUH? NICKNAME?! I, UH, WELL...

SO WHAT WAS YOUR NICKNAME?

I'VE EVEN WON A 5-ON-1!

I DIDN'T REALLY HAVE A NICKNAME...

YEAH, IT'S TOTALLY NORMAL.

THAT'S RIGHT! YOU CAN'T BE, SAY, "SUZUKI FROM 4TH." THAT JUST AIN'T **SCARY.**

YOU GOTTA BE SOMETHING LIKE, "THE FIREBALL OF 2ND," OR "THE MONSTER FROM 3RD."

NOW WAIT JUST A DAMN MINUTE! WHO SAYS YOU HAFTA HAVE A NICKNAME?

MAN, YOU AIN'T NOBODY THEN.

OOF!

HEY! KAMIYAMA!

WHAM

NEXT TIME? WHEN THE HELL'S THAT?!

THANKS FOR TRYIN', BUT BETTER LUCK NEXT TIME.

HUH?

HMM, WHAT ABOUT THAT GUY?

YOU PROBABLY HAD A NICKNAME BACK IN MIDDLE SCHOOL, TOO. LIKE "WEENIE" OR "SPINELESS," RIGHT?

CAN I HELP YOU?

WELL, I WAS ALWAYS A FAIRLY UPSTANDING STUDENT...

YOU PROBABLY NEVER DID ANYTHING BAD, RIGHT?

THAT'S NO NICKNAME! IT'S JUST WHAT YOU **WERE**.

IN JUNIOR HIGH I WAS KNOWN AS "THE ERRAND BOY."

WELL, I SUPPOSE IT WASN'T A **VERY** BAD THING...

WHAT, DID YOU RING SOMEONE'S DOORBELL AND RUN OFF?

I CAN'T SEE **YOU** DOING ANYTHING REALLY BAD.

BUT... ON ONE OCCASION, I DID DO SOMETHING BAD.

AS SEEN ON "DOMINO: CHALLENGING THE GUINNESS BOOK"! Help wanted! Set up dominos! No experience necessary!

THERE WAS A TV PROGRAM ABOUT AN ATTEMPT TO BREAK THE WORLD RECORD IN DOMINO BUILDING, AND THEY WERE RECRUITING STUDENTS TO HELP SET UP THE DOMINOES, SO I APPLIED RIGHT AWAY...

IT WAS TWO YEARS AGO, IN THE SPRING. I WAS IN 8TH GRADE...

I GOTCHA... BODIES STARTED DROPPIN' BEFORE THE DOMINOS, RIGHT!

AFTER A WEEK, SOME PEOPLE BEGAN TO TIRE OUT. A COUPLE EVEN COLLAPSED.

IT WAS FAIRLY SIMPLE WORK...

AT FIRST I WAS THRILLED TO BE PART OF IT ALL.

I'M GOING TO **RUIN** THIS PROGRAM!

IT WAS THEN THAT I MADE UP MY MIND.

WHAT THE HECK AM I DOING THIS FOR?

FOR SOME REASON, AFTER ABOUT A MONTH I BECAME VERY IRRITABLE.

N-NO WAY! DON'T TELL ME YOU KNOCKED 'EM ALL DOWN RIGHT BEFORE THE EVENT!

I SNEAKED INTO THE WAREHOUSE WHERE THEY WERE SET UP...

ON THE DAY BEFORE THE BIG EVENT, ALL THE DOMINOS WERE IN PLACE...

rattle

THE WORLD RECORD AT THAT TIME WAS 37,042 DOMINOS...

HEY, DON'T FRICKIN' LEAD US ON LIKE THAT!

DAMN, YOU HAD ME GOIN'!

NO, I'D NEVER DO SOME-THING **THAT** OUTRA-GEOUS!

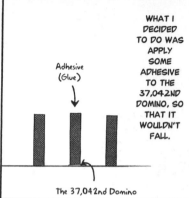

WHAT I DECIDED TO DO WAS APPLY SOME ADHESIVE TO THE 37,042ND DOMINO, SO THAT IT WOULDN'T FALL.

Adhesive (Glue)

The 37,042nd Domino

C'mon, somebody give me a nickname!

YOU ARE ONE INCREDIBLY BAD DUDE!!

OF COURSE, COMPARED TO ALL OF YOU, I'M SURE WHAT I DID WASN'T REALLY ALL THAT BAD...

NOTE: I MADE UP THE WORLD RECORD.

—16—

DEAR MOTHER...

IT'S ALREADY BEEN TWO MONTHS SINCE I ENROLLED AT CROMARTIE.

HOWEVER, I STILL FIND MYSELF UNABLE TO ADAPT TO THE ENVIRONMENT HERE...

BLGARGH!

YEARGH! I WANT A SMOKE!

I'M GONNA KILL YA, YA SON OF A BITCH!

THIS IS ME, RIGHT HERE.

IF I AM TO FIT IN AT THIS SCHOOL, I HAVE ONLY ONE OPTION AVAILABLE...

IN THE WORLD OF DELINQUENTS, THERE IS A REVOLUTIONARY PROGRAM, WHICH I LEARNED OF JUST THE OTHER DAY. IT'S KNOWN AS THE "HIGH SCHOOL DEBUT SYSTEM."

FOLLOWING THIS SET OF GUIDELINES, EVEN INDIVIDUALS WHO WERE OF A NORMAL SOCIAL STANDING IN JUNIOR HIGH SCHOOL CAN START OFF ON A NEW FOOT AS A DELINQUENT.

ADVICE FOR YOUR HIGH SCHOOL DEBUT

TO BE A TRUE HOODLUM, ONE MUST FIRST **LOOK** LIKE ONE. EVEN THOSE WHO ARE UNSKILLED IN FIGHTING CAN EASILY CHANGE THEIR APPEARANCE TO LOOK INTIMIDATING.

EITHER A POMPADOUR OR KINKY PERMANENT HAIRSTYLE WOULD BE IDEAL, HOWEVER BOTH ARE COSTLY AND REQUIRE A GREAT DEAL OF CARE. SHAVING THE HEAD IS ANOTHER OPTION, THOUGH NOT ADVISABLE FOR THOSE WITH A YOUTHFUL COUNTENANCE-- FOR HEREIN LIES THE DANGER OF RESEMBLING A YOUTH-LEAGUE BASEBALL PLAYER. FOR STARTERS, TRY BLEACHING YOUR HAIR BLONDE.

LESSON 1

20 MINUTES LATER

ALL RIGHT...

IF THIS DOES NOT LEND SUFFICIENT INTENSITY TO YOUR LOOK, TRY SHAVING YOUR EYEBROWS.

PLEASE NOTE THAT IF THE DYE IS LEFT ON FOR TOO LONG, IT MAY FULLY BLEACH YOUR HAIR WHITE.

DAMN...

CLENCH

FURROWING YOUR BROWS WILL ALSO HELP.

LIKE THIS, RIGHT?

HMM... THAT'S A BIT MORE LIKE IT.

10 MINUTES LATER

WHEW, THAT WAS A CLOSE ONE.

BY NOW YOU MAY BE FEELING TOUGHER, BUT DO NOT BE DECEIVED--YOU ARE STILL A WANNABE PUNK.

LESSON 2

IT ONLY TOOK A LITTLE EFFORT AND I'M ALREADY FEELING A LOT TOUGHER.

WOW, THIS IS REALLY SOMETHING.

THIS IS VERY INFORMATIVE...

DO NOT WEAR A BUTTON-DOWN SHIRT UNDER YOUR JACKET. INSTEAD, SHOW YOUR INDIVIDUALITY WITH A PRINTED SHIRT OR T-SHIRT.

P-CHK

GET INTO THE HABIT OF LEAVING YOUR COLLAR OPENED.

LESSON 3

WELL, YEAH! I DON'T GET IT!

YOU ARE PROBABLY WONDERING, "THEN WHAT'S THE POINT OF EVEN CARRYING A BAG?"

HUH? THEN WHAT'S THE POINT OF EVEN CARRYING A BAG?

DO NOT STORE TEXTBOOKS IN YOUR SATCHEL. ASSURE IT IS ALWAYS EMPTY AND FLAT.

LESSON 4

THWUMP

HMM... LESSON 5 SEEMS KIND OF TOUGH.

SEVER CONNECTIONS WITH YOUR FORMER, DILIGENT FRIENDS. ASSOCIATING WITH THEM WILL ONLY EXPOSE YOU. IGNORE THEM IF THEY SPEAK TO YOU.

LESSON 5

SO THAT'S IT! WHAT A CLEVER IDEA.

STORE A METAL PLATE IN YOUR BAG. IT WILL PROVE USEFUL IN BLOCKING AN OPPONENT'S PUNCHES.

IT'S AS IF I WERE BECOMING A **SPY**...

DISPOSE OF YOUR OLD PHOTOS, PARTICULARLY THOSE IN WHICH YOU ARE SMILING.

IF THIS PROVES TOO DIFFICULT, MEET THEM IN SECRET.

YOSHIDA

TABATA

I MEAN, I HAVE SOME REALLY CLOSE FRIENDS, LIKE YOSHIDA AND TABATA!

· · · · ·
· · · · ·

OKAY!

SCOOCH

AS FOR YOUR WALK-- SWAGGER AS LAZILY AS YOU CAN. IF YOU ARE STARED AT, RETURN THE LOOK WITH A MENACING GLARE.

LESSON 6

BWAOOOR

VWAAAM

INTERESTING... A LOT OF THIS COULD PROBABLY BE APPLIED TO EVERYDAY SOCIETY, NOT JUST THE DELINQUENT WORLD.

WALK AROUND WITH TOUGH-LOOKING FRIENDS WHENEVER POSSIBLE. (ON THAT NOTE, MAKE TOUGH-LOOKING FRIENDS.)

NOTE

GLARE

NOW FOR THE FINAL LESSON...

IF YOU'VE MADE IT THIS FAR, ONLY ONE STEP REMAINS BEFORE YOUR HIGH SCHOOL DEBUT.

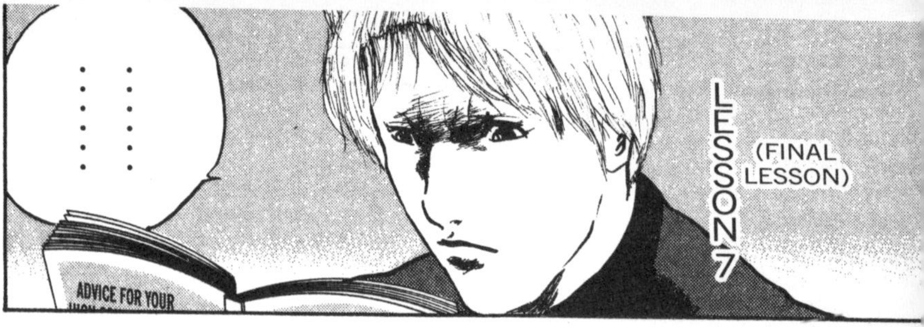
……
LESSON 7
(FINAL LESSON)
ADVICE FOR YOUR

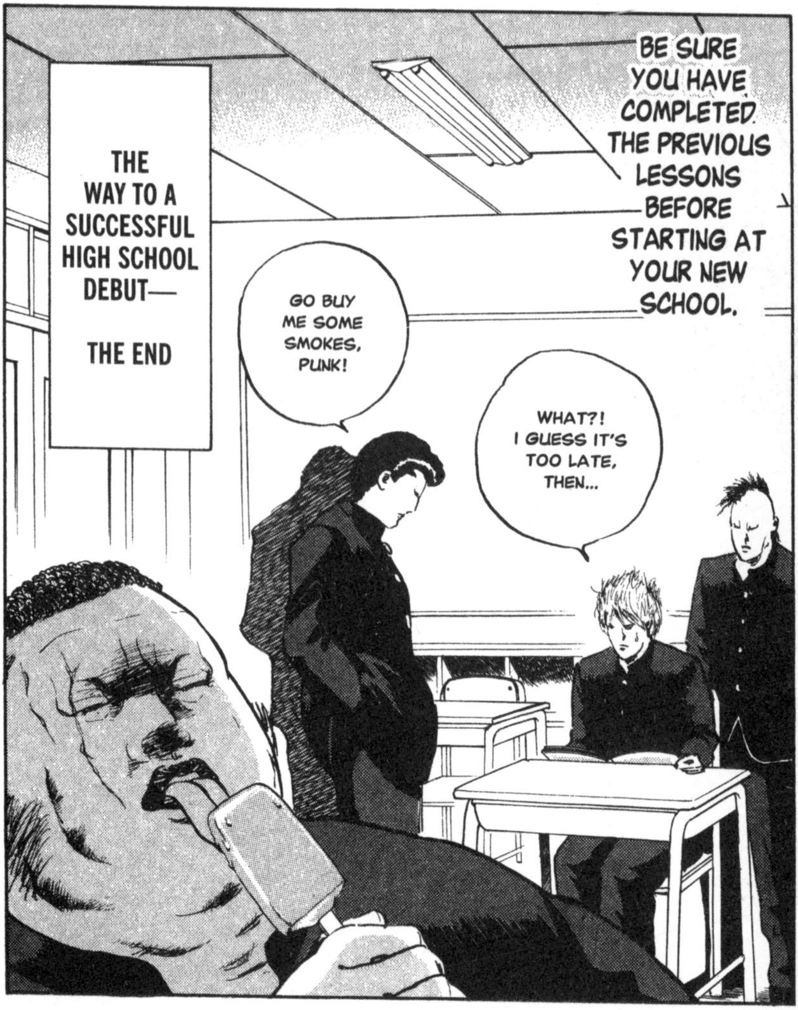
BE SURE YOU HAVE COMPLETED THE PREVIOUS LESSONS BEFORE STARTING AT YOUR NEW SCHOOL.
WHAT?! I GUESS IT'S TOO LATE, THEN...
GO BUY ME SOME SMOKES, PUNK!
THE WAY TO A SUCCESSFUL HIGH SCHOOL DEBUT—
THE END

ADVICE FOR YOUR HIGH SCHOOL DEBUT—IN STORES NEXT MONTH! (J/K)

YEAH. SINCE ALL OF US ARE SO, UH, **INDIVIDUALISTIC,** WE NEED A TOUGH SON OF A BITCH AT THE TOP TO KEEP THINGS GOIN' SMOOTH!

'BOUT TIME WE FIGURE OUT WHO'S THE STRONGEST IN OUR CLASS!

HOW THE HECK ARE WE GONNA DECIDE WHO'S THE STRONGEST?

NAH, I DON'T THINK THAT'S RIGHT...

DUNNO. BUT YEAH, PROLLY SUMPIN' LIKE THAT.

IN THE NORMAL SCHOOLS, THAT'D BE SOMETHIN' LIKE A **CLASS REP,** RIGHT?

I'LL INTRODUCE THEM NOW.

TO START WITH, WE PICKED A FEW MEN WHO HAVE SOLID FIGHTING RECORDS.

: : : :

IT'S THESE THREE.

THAT'S WHAT I WANNA KNOW! NOW SIDDOWN OR I'LL FRICKIN' KILL YA!

WHY HAVE I BEEN NOMINATED?

WAIT JUST A MINUTE.

PROTAGONIST, TAKASHI KAMIYAMA

ALL OF US HAVE GOTTEN USED TO BEING HOODS. NOW, WHEN YOU SEE SOMEONE WHO LOOKS REAL BAD OR REAL STRONG, IT DOESN'T SCARE YA AS MUCH AS IT USED TO.

HAYA-SHIDA! **YOU** DID?

I NOMINATED KAMIYAMA.

IT'S LIKE THIS. SAY THERE WAS A **RABBIT**, AND IT WAS LIVING WITH A BUNCH OF LIONS, AND GETTING ALONG JUST FINE... THAT'D HAVE TO BE ONE BADASS RABBIT.

AIN'T THAT KIND OF A **STRETCH**?

ON THE OTHER HAND, A TOTALLY NORMAL-LOOKIN' GUY LIKE KAMIYAMA HERE LOOKS THREATENING AS HELL.

I'M NOT SO SURE I FOLLOW.

I WANNA SEE THE DEVIL THAT'S HIDING IN **YOU**!

WHAT I'M SAYIN' IS...

I GET IT! DAMN, THAT RABBIT **ROCKS**!

DAMN STRAIGHT! A FISTFIGHT'S THE ONLY WAY!

THEY GOTTA DUKE IT OUT!

SO THEN... HOW DO WE DECIDE WHO'S THE STRONGEST?

HEY, WAIT A MINUTE! THERE'S THREE OF 'EM. THAT MEANS TWO WOULD FIGHT, THEN THE WINNER OF THAT MATCH WOULD HAVE TO TAKE ON THE LAST GUY!

BUT I THINK I READ SOMEWHERE THAT WHAT KIND OF SHAPE YOU'RE IN CAN VARY A LITTLE BIT DAY BY DAY, SO IT ISN'T ALWAYS THE **STRONGEST** WHO WINS A FIGHT.

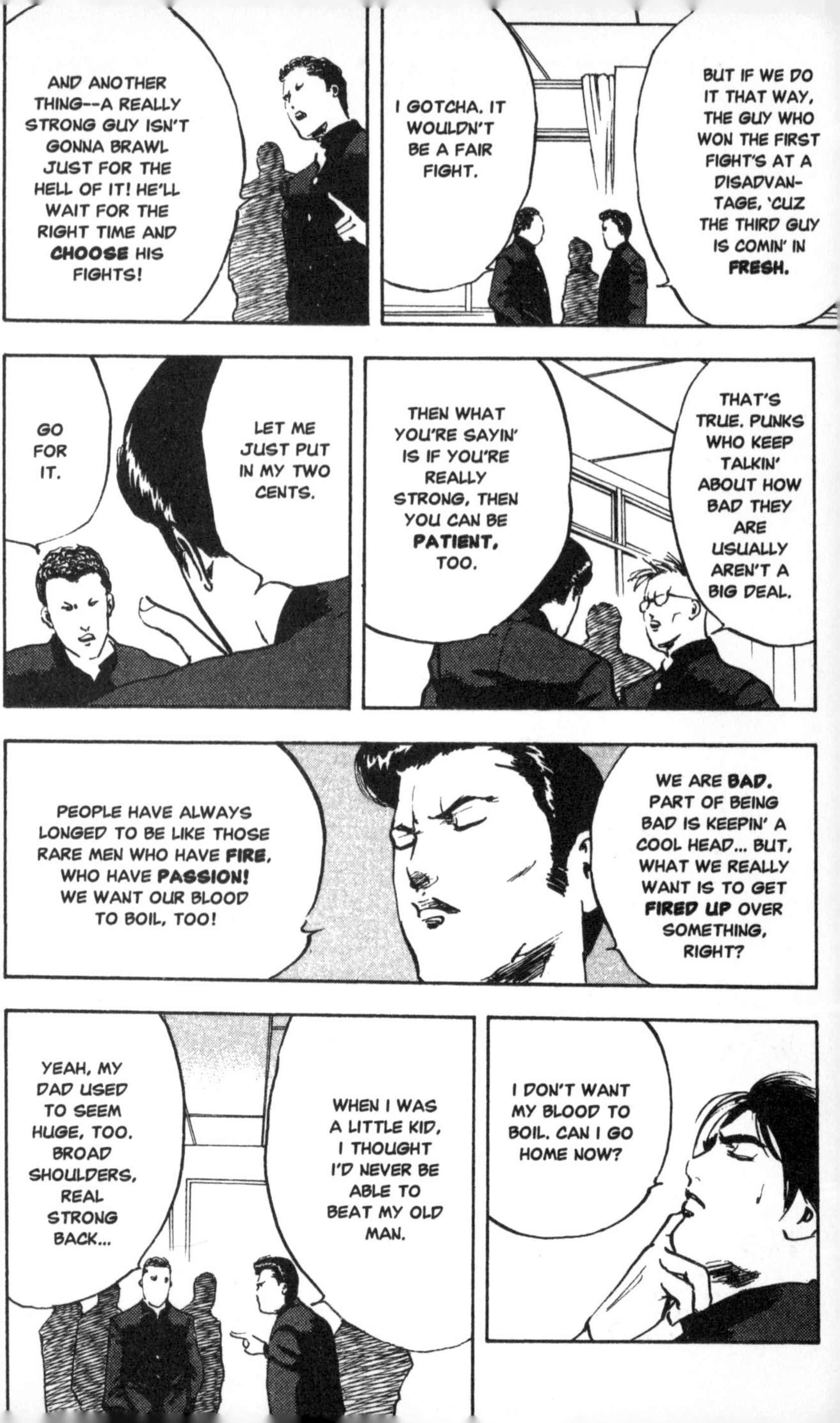
AND ANOTHER THING--A REALLY STRONG GUY ISN'T GONNA BRAWL JUST FOR THE HELL OF IT! HE'LL WAIT FOR THE RIGHT TIME AND CHOOSE HIS FIGHTS!
I GOTCHA. IT WOULDN'T BE A FAIR FIGHT.
BUT IF WE DO IT THAT WAY, THE GUY WHO WON THE FIRST FIGHT'S AT A DISADVANTAGE, 'CUZ THE THIRD GUY IS COMIN' IN FRESH.
GO FOR IT.
LET ME JUST PUT IN MY TWO CENTS.
THEN WHAT YOU'RE SAYIN' IS IF YOU'RE REALLY STRONG, THEN YOU CAN BE PATIENT, TOO.
THAT'S TRUE. PUNKS WHO KEEP TALKIN' ABOUT HOW BAD THEY ARE USUALLY AREN'T A BIG DEAL.
PEOPLE HAVE ALWAYS LONGED TO BE LIKE THOSE RARE MEN WHO HAVE FIRE, WHO HAVE PASSION! WE WANT OUR BLOOD TO BOIL, TOO!
WE ARE BAD. PART OF BEING BAD IS KEEPIN' A COOL HEAD... BUT, WHAT WE REALLY WANT IS TO GET FIRED UP OVER SOMETHING, RIGHT?
YEAH, MY DAD USED TO SEEM HUGE, TOO. BROAD SHOULDERS, REAL STRONG BACK...
WHEN I WAS A LITTLE KID, I THOUGHT I'D NEVER BE ABLE TO BEAT MY OLD MAN.
I DON'T WANT MY BLOOD TO BOIL. CAN I GO HOME NOW?

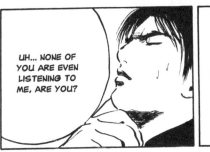

UH... NONE OF YOU ARE EVEN LISTENING TO ME, ARE YOU?

SO THE TOUGHEST GUY IN OUR CLASS HAS TO HAVE A STRONG BACK TOO, HUH?

WE HAVE TO SEE IF THERE'S SUCH A "MAN AMONG MEN" IN **OUR** CLASS! IT'S A QUESTION OF **PRIDE**!

WE'RE LOOKING FOR A REAL PATIENT DUDE, WHO'S GOT A STRONG BACK, AND HAS "THIS FIRE." HMM. AIN'T SO EASY...

OKAY, LET'S SEE WHAT WE GOT...

WE SHOULD CHECK IT OUT!

I HEARD THE FRESHMEN IN CLASS 1-2 ARE TRYIN' TO SEE WHO'S **THEIR** STRONGEST.

THEN ALL WE NEED NOW IS TO COME UP WITH SOME KINDA TEST!

OKAY!

WHAT THE HELL?!

HEY! DID YA FIGURE OUT WHO'S THE TOUGHEST IN YER CLASS YET?

RATTLE

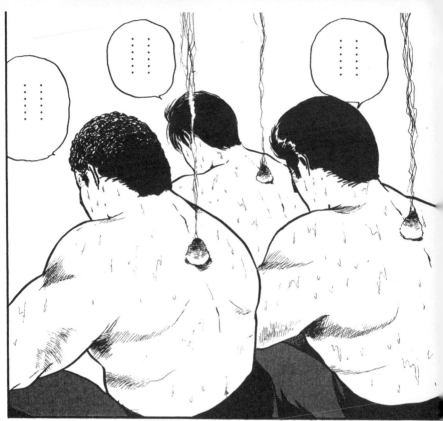

I DUNNO. SOMEHOW THIS DOESN'T SEEM RIGHT...

I.... I WON!

I CAN'T TAKE ANY MORE!

DAMN, THAT THING'S HOT!

YOU GOT THE WRONG IDEA.

⬆ TAKASHI KAMIYAMA

This manga's main character, as you are no doubt aware. His motto is, "Perseverance, self-reliance, and no pretenses." He was a diligent and able honors student throughout junior high, though he now stands out quite a bit among the ruffians of Cromartie. On occasion he may seem to behave rather strangely, and you might wonder if he isn't the dumbest one of all. However, Kamiyama's occasional weirdness may have done the trick, as he adjusted to life at Cromartie High before anyone even realized it. His adaptive abilities are beyond amazing. The next thing you know, he even has his own faction, the "Kamiyama Corps." One time, he tried bleaching his hair, and it seemed as though he'd go astray, but he ended up sticking to his original, illustrious and critically acclaimed image. Throughout the story you will often see him in the process of writing letters to his mother. This has led to the theory that he and his mother live apart, but in fact the author merely wanted to use the phrase "Dear (so and so)," and did not consider the implications. One may go so far as to say that Kamiyama as the main character could instill courage within persecuted students all over the country... Yeah, right!

SHINJIROU HAYASHIDA

Taken from my other manga, **Kachou Baka Ichidai,** he has undergone the transformation from businessman to hoodlum high school student. I therefore had to refine his stupidity a bit. You could say he's commander of my shock troops, always leading the charge, but I'd rather he *not* lead the charge. If you were to liken the "World of Nonaka" to the **Star Wars** universe, you could say that Hayashida and Maeda here are like my R2-D2 and C3-PO. Hmm, so does that make Kamiyama a young Anakin? Whoa, this is working out pretty well! Later on it will be proven that his intelligence is even lower than a chimpanzee's. The most charming thing about him is his B-grade mohawk. His motto is, "No Future."

AKIRA MAEDA

This is another character taken from **Kachou Baka Ichidai.** His motto is "With friends like these, who needs enemies?" Unfortunately, he has no nickname. He's a fairly capable fighter, and not stupid either, but for some reason everyone seems to walk all over him. However, this witty "straight man" has earned himself a reputation as well as many closet fans. He is the only level-headed character in the story; if it weren't for his composure, I imagine the level of stupidity in this book would've been as out of control as a runaway train. Maeda is always the subject of Hayashida's and Kamiyama's torment. He'll bring a smile to your face while earning your sympathy. He is renowned for the startling resemblance he bears to his mother. His most charming feature is his thin and wispy eyebrows.

UM... SURE, NO PROBLEM.

HEY, TANAKA! WHY DON'T YOU GO GET ME SOME SWEET ROLLS?

UH, OKAY... SURE THING.

CUP OF RAMEN FOR ME! MAKE SURE YOU PUT THE HOT WATER IN IT, TOO.

GET ME A PORK SANDWICH AND MILK.

HUH?

PAT

YAKISOBA, A BIG ONE FOR ME!

UH... OKAY.

AND GET **ME** SOME BREAD!

ONCE I WAS JUST LIKE YOU, RUNNING AROUND AS EVERYONE'S **ERRAND BOY.**

BUT THAT'D ONLY MAKE THEM MAD!

DON'T DO IT, TANAKA-KUN.

HEY, CUT OUT THE DAMN SOAP OPERA OVER THERE!

WELL... I GUESS SO, BUT...

IT WILL BE DIFFICULT AT FIRST, BUT YOU'LL PREVAIL. AND THEN YOU'LL BE ON YOUR WAY TO ADULTHOOD.

BUT THEN I MET SOMEONE WHOSE SUPPORT AND ADVICE GAVE ME THE COURAGE TO SAY **"NO."**

FINE, THEN. SOUNDS GOOD TO ME.

WELL, IF YOU ABSOLUTELY INSIST, **I'LL** GO INSTEAD.

OH, YEAH? WHO'S GONNA GO BUY OUR FOOD THEN, HUH?!

TANAKA-KUN HAS TURNED OVER A NEW LEAF. HE'S NOT GOING TO BE YOUR **CHUMP** ANY LONGER.

OKAY.

UM... PIZZA POCKET AND STRAWBERRY MILK, PLEASE.

ICED CAFE AU LAIT FOR ME.

MELON ROLL AND COFFEE.

ALL RIGHT.

EGG SALAD SANDWICH FOR ME.

I'LL HAVE A JELLY ROLL.

I'M SURE THEY WILL COME TO REALIZE THE FOOLISHNESS OF THEIR WAYS!

HOWEVER, I AM SOMEWHAT SURPRISED THAT EVEN TANAKA-KUN PUT IN A REQUEST.

I GUESS THIS ISN'T SUCH A BIG DEAL.

IT SEEMS THEY'RE DEMANDING MORE AND MORE EVERY DAY.

THE AMOUNT OF FOOD THEY REQUEST HAS INCREASED TENFOLD.

ONE MONTH LATER.

SOMETHIN' ON YOUR MIND? YOU CAN TELL ME.

HIRAI-SAN (17) Forced to repeat the 10th grade, he does not mix well with his new classmates. He's happy to talk to just about anyone.

AREN'T YOU HIRAI-SAN THE FLUNKER?

HUH?

HEY, WHAT'S UP?

HUH?

MAYBE YOU'RE SELLING YOURSELF SHORT.

AH, I DON'T KNOW WHAT TO DO! AT THIS RATE, I WON'T GET ANY STUDYING DONE--OR EVEN BE ABLE TO GO **HOME,** FOR THAT MATTER!

BUT YOU CAN'T RELY ON OTHER PEOPLE TO SOLVE YOUR PROBLEMS FOR YA! TRY HAVING A LITTLE FAITH IN **YOURSELF!** IF YOU DON'T HAVE THE BRAWN, THEN USE YOUR **HEAD!**

LISTEN, DON'T THINK I'M TALKIN' TO YA JUST BECAUSE I FLUNKED 1ST YEAR, AND GOT NO FRIENDS, AND TURNED INTO SOME KINDA LONER...

HIRAI-SAN REALLY CHEERED ME UP. ONLY, IT'S TOO BAD HE ADDED TO THE ORDER LIST.

GO GET 'EM. AND WHILE YOU'RE AT IT, GET **ME** A BAG OF KELP DROPS.

THANK YOU VERY MUCH. PERHAPS I WAS UNDER-ESTIMATING MYSELF SOMEWHAT.

A FOOD STAND!

· · ·
· · ·

WHAT TO DO... HOW CAN I END THE BULLYING? HOW CAN I LIBERATE MYSELF FROM THIS *HARDSHIP?*

I CAN SET UP MY STOCK RIGHT HERE IN THE CLASSROOM. IT WOULD SAVE ME THE TIME OF GOING OUT AND FILLING THE ORDERS ONE BY ONE.

YES, I SAW SOMETHING ABOUT IT ON TV! BUYING IN BULK WILL REDUCE MY OVERALL COSTS.

AFTER ALL THE FANCY TALK, HE'S JUST A **CHUMP** AFTER ALL.

THINK I'LL SEND KAMIYAMA OUT TO GET ME SOMETHIN'.

MAN, I'M THIRSTY...

HUH?!

RATTLE

HEY, KAMIYAMA! GO BUY ME A...

HM?

SALE
Special discount on all items!

PLEASE WAIT IN LINE, SIR!

GEE, THAT **IS** PRETTY CHEAP...

low price

WELCOME TO PUSHOVER KAMIYAMA'S, WHERE OUR MOTTO IS "THE BEST DEAL YOU CAN GET ANY-WHERE!"

WHAT THE HELL IS THIS?

TANAKA-KUN! TODAY WE'RE OFFERING 20% OFF ALL ITEMS!

HEY, KAMI-YAMA-KUN!

THIS MAN SOUNDS LIKE A **PRO!**

WELCOME! WOULD YOU LIKE SOME MILK TO GO WITH THAT?

YOU'RE THE REAL SERIOUS TYPE. YOU GET **FOCUSED** ON SOMETHING AND THEN FORGET ABOUT EVERYTHING ELSE.

I DIDN'T COME HERE TO BUY ANYTHING. ACTUALLY... THERE'S SOMETHING I WANTED TO TALK TO YOU ABOUT.

YOU'VE LOST SIGHT OF SOMETHING **IMPORTANT!** I WANT YOU TO REMEMBER WHAT THAT IS!

WHAT COULD POSSIBLY BE WEIRD ABOUT **ME?!**

LOW PRICE KING

SHOPLIFTING PROHIBITED!

SO I'LL PUT IT TO YOU STRAIGHT-- YOU'RE HEADED IN A REALLY WEIRD DIRECTION!

I'M JUST GLAD YOU UNDER- STAND NOW.

THANKS SO MUCH, TANAKA- KUN! IF IT WEREN'T FOR YOU, I MIGHT HAVE LOST IT ALL!

TH... THAT'S IT!

HMM... SOME- THING IMPOR- TANT, HUH?

THAT IS ONE BAD MOTHER...

NO, IT'S NOT **THAT!**

I HAD COMPLETELY FORGOTTEN TO ADD THE **SALES TAX!**

NO MATTER HOW YOU LOOK AT IT, HE AIN'T NO CHUMP.

CHAPTER SIX: **ROCK YOU**

BUT THAT SENTIMENT WAS MET WITH RIDICULE. IT SEEMED CROMARTIE WAS DETERMINED TO CONTINUE ON ITS SELF-DESTRUCTIVE COURSE.

KAMIYAMA'S DESIRE TO CLEAN UP THE SCHOOL ONLY GREW STRONGER AS THE DAYS WENT BY.

HAYA-SHIDA-KUN.

NO WAY, NO HOW.

STILL, I KNOW THAT IF I KEEP TRYING, I WILL SEE THE LIGHT EVENTUALLY!

PROTAGONIST: TAKASHI KAMIYAMA

WHO DO YOU MEAN?

WELL, IF YOU COULD BEAT **HIM**, THEN MAYBE THINGS WOULD CHANGE AROUND HERE. BUT THAT AIN'T GONNA HAPPEN.

I DON'T MEAN TO ARGUE. TRUE, GIVING UP IS EASY ENOUGH, BUT WHAT GOOD WOULD IT DO US?

· · ·
· · ·
· · ·

WELL, WHY HASN'T HIRAI-SAN DONE ANYTHING ABOUT IT?

ANOTHER FIRST YEAR IN CLASS 1-3. THE GUY'S UNBELIEVABLE! I'M TELLIN' YA, AS LONG AS HE'S HERE, EVERY DAY IS GONNA BE LIKE SOME KINDA BADASS OLYMPICS.

I DON'T BELIEVE IT! AN OPPONENT EVEN HIRAI-SAN THE FLUNKER WOULD TURN TAIL TO?!

WHAT?!

I'M NOT GONNA SAY IT OUT LOUD, BUT... EVEN HIRAI-SAN THE FLUNKER IS SCARED. HE'S BEEN TRYING TO AVOID FIGHTING THE GUY.

YOU MEAN YOU DON'T **KNOW?** IF I DON'T KNOW HIS NAME, HOW ON EARTH AM I SUPPOSED TO FIND HIM?

I, UH, COULDN'T TELL YA.

WELL, I'D AT LEAST LIKE TO GO GET A LOOK AT THIS GUY. WHAT'S HIS NAME?

GO THERE, AND I'LL SEE? WHAT DOES THAT MEAN?

HUH?

JUST GO THERE. YOU'LL SEE.

RATTLE

FIRST YEAR, CLASS 3... THIS IS THE PLACE!

1-3

I'VE HAD SO MANY RUN-INS WITH GUYS LIKE THIS THAT THEY DON'T EVEN SCARE ME ANYMORE.

I DON'T SEE ANYTHING *THAT* BAD HERE.

THERE CERTAINLY ARE A LOT OF BADASSES GATHERED HERE, BUT I'M USED TO THEIR KIND...

THIS IS A WASTE OF TIME.

I'M HEADING BACK.

IN FACT, NOW I FEEL LIKE I MIGHT EVEN BE ABLE TO BEAT SOME OF THEM IN A FIGHT.

RATTLE

THERE'S NO SUCH GUY HERE.

THIS IS CLASS 1-3.

HAYA-SHIDA-KUN MUST HAVE BEEN MIS-TAKEN.

THAT'S HIM!

IS THIS GUY **REALLY** A HIGH SCHOOL STUDENT?

THERE'S NO DOUBT ABOUT IT! STILL... THERE'S SOMETHING ABOUT HIM THAT'S BUGGING ME.

UH, HI... I'M KAMIYAMA, FROM CLASS 1-2.

AND FOR THAT MATTER, CAN HE EVEN SPEAK JAPANESE?!

HE WON'T EVEN REVEAL HIS IDENTITY? OR COULD IT BE HE DOESN'T UNDERSTAND JAPANESE AFTER ALL?

: : : :

UM... WHAT'S YOUR NAME?

THE...THE *TEACHER'S* HERE?!

RATTLE

ALL RIGHT. TIME FOR CLASS, EVERYONE.

THIS GUY ISN'T THE TEACHER EITHER!

THEN THAT MEANS...

WELL, EVEN IF HE *WAS* THE TEACHER, THAT WOULD BE AN ENTIRELY DIFFERENT PROBLEM. WHO THE HECK IS THIS GUY? AND WHERE DID HE COME FROM?

MY SINGLE REMAINING HOPE HAS BEEN DASHED. I THOUGHT PERHAPS HE MIGHT HAVE BEEN THE *TEACHER...*

BEFORE I ATTEMPT TO FIGHT HIM, I MUST FIRST RESOLVE THE ISSUE OF EXACTLY **WHAT** THIS MAN IS.

THIS LEAVES ME NO CHOICE BUT TO SIT IN ON A CLASS WITH HIM.

HE... HE'S RAISING HIS HAND!

WHOA!

SO BE IT. ACADEMICS IS MY SPECIALTY. I'LL ANSWER BEFORE HIM! THINK YOU'LL BEAT ME, DO YOU...

BUT CLASS BEGAN NOT **5 MINUTES** AGO! WHAT AMAZING VIGILANCE... FAR BEYOND THE NORM, TO BE SURE!

Going to the bath-room →

RATTLE

HUH?

UH... WE'RE IN THE MIDDLE OF A **TEST**, YOU KNOW.

HERE! HERE! HEEERE!

...SO, WHO IS THIS FELLA?

HE'S A TRULY FEARSOME INDIVIDUAL (OR SO IT SEEMS).

FREDDIE →

A NEW OPPONENT HAS APPEARED BEFORE US. HIS NAME IS FREDDIE... (WE DON'T KNOW HIS REAL NAME, SO WE DECIDED TO CALL HIM THAT.)

THE THREE HAVE MET TO DISCUSS "THE OVERTHROW OF FREDDIE."

I BELIEVE IT'S NECESSARY TO **KNOW** YOUR ENEMY BEFORE ATTEMPTING TO FIGHT HIM.

SO IS HE A STUDENT OR NOT?

HE TRANSFERRED HERE LAST MONTH. SEEMS HIS NAME ISN'T ON THE CLASS ROSTER, THOUGH.

WE'RE ONLY HIGH SCHOOL STUDENTS. I DOUBT WE'LL BE ABLE TO GATHER A LOT OF INFORMATION ON OUR OWN. FOR NOW, WE SHOULD STICK WITH LEARNING THE BASICS.

AKIRA MAEDA (No nickname)

ALL ANYONE REALLY KNOWS ABOUT HIM IS THAT HE'S GOT ONE **HAIRY** CHEST!

RIGHT... THEN WE'LL NEED TO DO MORE RESEARCH ON THIS FREDDIE, RIGHT?

YES, WE SHOULD FIND OUT WHATEVER WE'RE ABLE TO.

BLOOD TYPE, EH?

I don't get it, but okay.

WE SHOULD START WITH HIS BLOOD TYPE! I'M PRETTY GOOD WITH THAT KINDA STUFF, SO I BET I CAN FIGURE OUT WHAT HE IS.

YEAH. HE'S READING A TEXTBOOK.

IS HE IN THERE?

1-3

HARD-WORKING STUDENTS TEND TO BE B-TYPES.

HE'S MORE **STUDIOUS** THAN I HAD EXPECTED.

Have his sideburns grown?

HE'S HOLDING THE TEXTBOOK **UPSIDE DOWN!**

MATHEMATICS

NO, WAIT! TAKE A CLOSER LOOK!

WH... WHAT'S THIS, NOW?

WHAT'S GOING ON?!

CARELESS? WAS HE EVEN READING TO BEGIN WITH?

WELL, AB-TYPES **ARE** OFTEN CARELESS!

IIG STARTED TO DO PUSHUPS ALL OF A SUDDEN!

HE ALREADY COL-LAPSED!

WHAT NOW?

OH! LOOK!

GET OUTTA HERE!

SUDDEN PUSHUPS STRONGLY SUGGEST AN A-TYPE!

BLOOD TYPE BOOK

OH, FREDDIE! YOU'VE GOT NO STAMINA!

BUT HE WAS ONLY ON HIS **FIRST** PUSHUP!

HUH?! WHAT THE HECK?

IF IT COVERS **SUDDENLY DOING PUSHUPS,** THEN WHY WOULDN'T IT MENTION "LACK OF STAMINA" OR SOMETHING?

HMM, LET ME SEE. GUYS WITH NO STAMINA... SORRY, MAN. IT DOESN'T SAY ANYTHING ABOUT THAT.

HAYA-SHIDA-KUN, WHAT BLOOD TYPE ARE PEOPLE WITH NO STAMINA?

HAYA-SHIDA-KUN! WHAT DOES IT SAY ABOUT *TEPPO* PRACTICE?

SLAP

HE... HE'S DOING SUMO *TEPPO* PRACTICE!!

WHERE THE HELL DID YOU BUY THAT BOOK?

IF HE'S DOIN' *TEPPO,* HE'S AN A-TYPE FOR SURE!

SO WHAT'S THE BIG DEAL?

HE'S PUTTING HIS BOOKS AWAY!

WHAT'S HE DOING NOW?

WHOA, **NOW** LOOK!

HE'S GOING HOME--EVEN THOUGH IT'S ONLY **2ND PERIOD!**

RATTLE

You aren't just taking a guess?

WHAT? ARE YOU SERIOUS?!

I'VE GOT IT.

I THOUGHT WE COULD FIGURE OUT HIS BLOOD TYPE... BUT THIS IS HARDER THAN I THOUGHT.

He's a tough nut to crack.

HIS MOVEMENTS ARE COMPLETELY UNPREDICTABLE.

BASED ON STATISTICS, THERE'S A 67% CHANCE FREDDIE'S BLOOD TYPE IS B!!

BLOOD TYPE BOOK

GOOD STUDY HABITS, BUT CARELESS... FURTHERMORE, HE'S PRONE TO SUDDEN PUSHUPS AND SUMO EXERCISES. WITH THIS COMBINATION OF TRAITS...

BLOOD TYPE BOOK

HOW ABOUT THAT...

TYPE B, HUH?

SO THAT'S IT, THEN!

TYPE B?!

FREDDIE ALREADY WENT HOME.

THE BUS CARRYING THESE HOT BLOODED **BADASSES** IS EN ROUTE TO NIKKO.

THE CROMARTIE STUDENTS ARE GOING ON A FIELD TRIP.

HIS NAME— YUTAKA TAKENOUCHI (16).

ONE MAN SITS QUIETLY IN THE BACK OF THE BUS.

BUT, DESPITE ALL THAT, I STILL HAVE ONE BIG PROBLEM...

I STAY BEHIND THE SCENES, BUT I'M THE ONE WHO'S IN CHARGE OF THE 1ST YEARS AT CROMARTIE. NO ONE IS MORE RESPECTED, AND WHEN IT COMES TO FIGHTING ABILITY, NO ONE CAN HOLD A CANDLE TO ME, NOBODY GETS IN MY WAY, NOT EVEN THE 3RD YEARS.

WHENEVER I SEE THOSE OLD TEMPLES, I FEEL IMMERSED IN ELEGANCE.

urp

BUT I LOVE GOING ON TRIPS, SO THERE'S NO WAY I'D SIT ONE OUT. ESPECIALLY IF IT'S TO NIKKO.

I GET MOTION SICK REAL EASY.

URP...

WE BETTER STAY CLEAR OF HIM TODAY.

DAMN, SOMETHIN' MUST'VE REALLY GOTTEN TO HIM!

WHOA, WHAT'S WITH TAKENOUCHI? CHECK OUT HIS FACE!

He looks PISSED!

NOT THAT I'M TRYIN' TO BRAG, BUT I'VE NEVER PUKED, NOT EVEN ONCE.

EVER SINCE ELEMENTARY SCHOOL I'VE BEEN ABLE TO GET BY ON GUTS ALONE.

GEE, NOBODY'S SITTING IN THE BACK...

HUH?

HEY, AREN'T THERE ANY FREE SEATS LEFT?

Will not ease the pain! Oh, Cromartie, our dear Cromartie High!

Fleeting comfort...

It's field trip day, so Kamiyama is in high spirits.

UMPH! THERE WE GO!

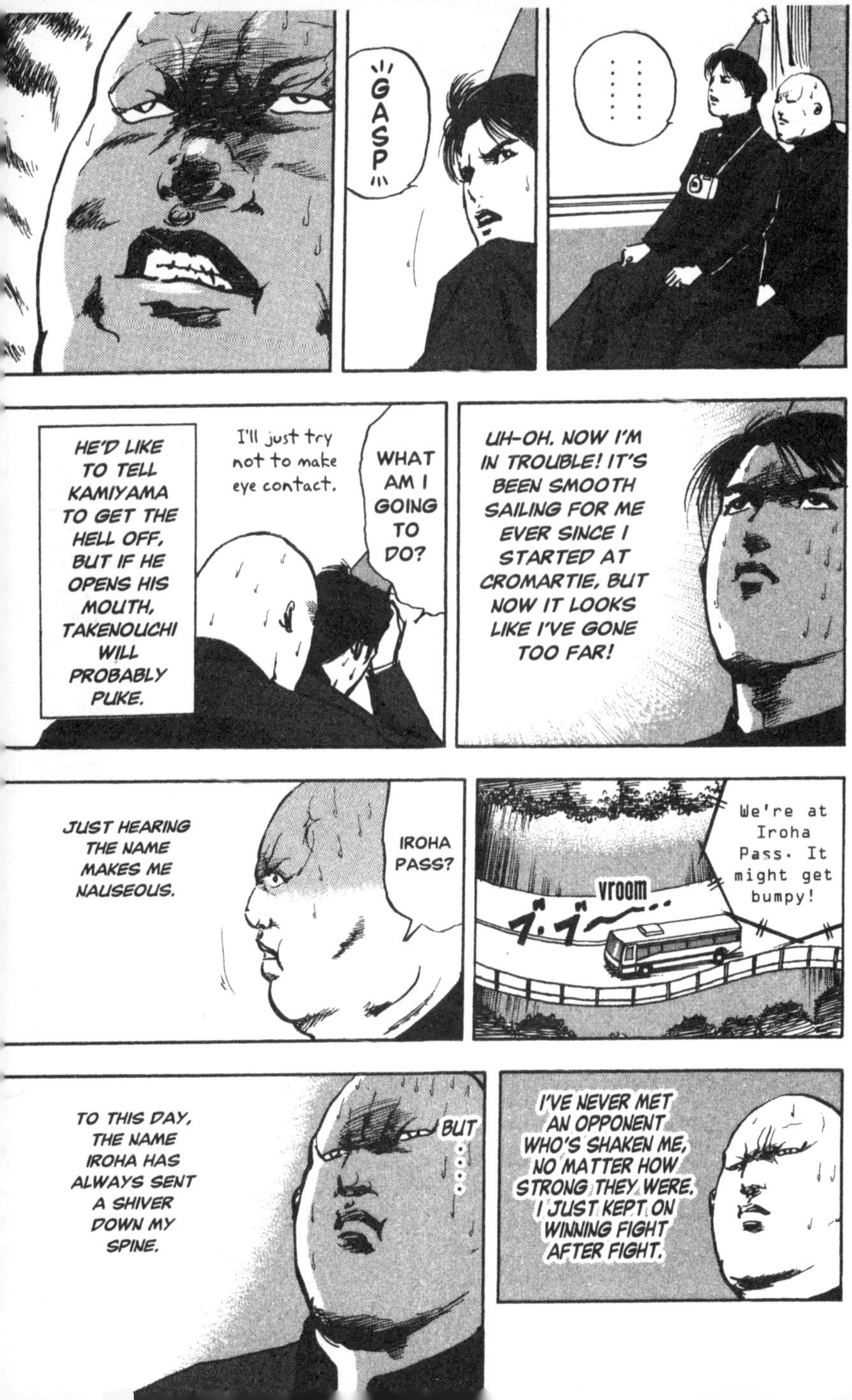
......
GASP
UH-OH. NOW I'M IN TROUBLE! IT'S BEEN SMOOTH SAILING FOR ME EVER SINCE I STARTED AT CROMARTIE, BUT NOW IT LOOKS LIKE I'VE GONE TOO FAR!
WHAT AM I GOING TO DO?
I'll just try not to make eye contact.
HE'D LIKE TO TELL KAMIYAMA TO GET THE HELL OFF, BUT IF HE OPENS HIS MOUTH, TAKENOUCHI WILL PROBABLY PUKE.
We're at Iroha Pass. It might get bumpy!
vroom
IROHA PASS?
JUST HEARING THE NAME MAKES ME NAUSEOUS.
I'VE NEVER MET AN OPPONENT WHO'S SHAKEN ME, NO MATTER HOW STRONG THEY WERE. I JUST KEPT ON WINNING FIGHT AFTER FIGHT.
BUT....
TO THIS DAY, THE NAME IROHA HAS ALWAYS SENT A SHIVER DOWN MY SPINE.

OH! THAT'S RIGHT!

WHAT A PICKLE! I AM REALLY IN FOR IT NOW!

UH... WHEN DOES THIS **MONKEY** PLAN TO GET OFF OF ME?

Please hold on around these turns, everyone.

scree

THE SON OF A BITCH... WHEN WE GET OFF THIS BUS, I SWEAR I'M GONNA FRICKIN' *KILL HIM!!*

GET THE HELL OFF!

I SUPPOSE IT WAS RATHER **UNCOURTEOUS** OF ME NOT TO REMOVE MY HAT.

EXCUSE ME! THE BUS TURNED SUDDENLY, AND...

URGH...

thwump

OOF!

WELL, I DO HAVE A LOT OF ENEMIES. IT WOULDN'T BE UNUSUAL IF **SOMEBODY** WERE TARGETING ME.

NO DOUBT ABOUT IT! KAMIYAMA'S OUT TO TAKE MY LIFE!

IN THAT INSTANT KAMIYAMA'S EYES LOOKED LIKE THOSE OF A KILLER.

I GOT ENOUGH STRENGTH TO TAKE CARE OF YOU, PAL!

MAYBE SOME BUMS FROM ANOTHER SCHOOL SENT HIM. BUT YOU KNOW WHAT, KAMIYAMA? I'M NOT IN CHARGE OF THIS CLASS FOR NOTHIN'.

OKAY, YOU WIN... JUST LET GO OF ME, PLEASE!

UNGH... RP.

sway sway

YOU DON'T LOOK WELL! HANG IN THERE!

THAT'S RIGHT! I'M CARSICK! DON'T ACT LIKE YOU DON'T FRICKIN' KNOW ALREADY!

TAKENOUCHI-SAN, DON'T TELL ME YOU'RE...

BUT DON'T WORRY. I HAVE JUST THE THING FOR THIS KIND OF SITUATION!

I'M SO TERRIBLY SORRY. I DID NOT MEAN TO BE SO INSENSITIVE!

YOU MUST BE HUNGRY. I BROUGHT SOME SNACKS WITH ME. IT MIGHT BE A LITTLE WARM, THOUGH.

...

PLEASE, GO AHEAD AND EAT THIS PUDDING.

BWRGH!

COME ON, EVERYONE! LET'S ENJOY NIKKO!

honk-honk ピーポー ピーポー

AFTER EATING **PUDDING?** WHAT THE HELL?

I HEARD TAKENOUCHI PASSED OUT AFTER EATIN' SOME PUDDIN'.

BET THAT WAS ONE MEAN PUDDIN'.

—54—

CHAPTER NINE: **TAXI**

YUTAKA TAKENOUCHI (16)

CURRENTLY THE BOSS OF CROMARTIE'S 1ST YEAR CLASS... NO ONE IS MORE RESPECTED, AND WHEN IT COMES TO FIGHTING ABILITY, NO ONE CAN HOLD A CANDLE TO HIM.

NOBODY GETS IN HIS WAY, NOT EVEN THE THIRD YEAR STUDENTS. DESPITE THAT, HE HAS ONE WEAKNESS, AND THAT IS...

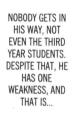

WHAT? BASS?

TAKENOUCHI-KUN! I HAVE AWFUL NEWS! MAEDA'S BEEN KIDNAPPED BY A GANG FROM BASS HIGH SCHOOL.

BUT IT AIN'T GOT ANYTHING TO DO WITH HOW **TOUGH** I AM!

HE IS PREDISPOSED TO BECOME MOTION SICK VERY EASILY.

I'VE GOTTEN INTO IT WITH THOSE BASS PANSIES A COUPLE TIMES BEFORE. I'D BE FINE EVEN ON MY OWN.

SHOULD WE GO ROUND UP THE TROOPS?

I'M FUNDAMENTALLY AGAINST FIGHTING, BUT... SINCE A **FRIEND** IS IN TROUBLE, IT'S A NECESSARY EVIL!

OKAY! WE'RE ALL SET!

GET MOVIN', YOU TWO!

CERTAINLY SOMEONE WE CAN DEPEND ON!

MAN, TAKE-NOUCHI'S SOME-THIN' ELSE.

IT'S ALRIGHT. PLEASE, AFTER YOU!

THEY'RE PROBABLY KNOCKING HIM SENSELESS. THERE'S NO TIME TO LOSE!

WHY DON'T WE JUST WALK? IT'S NOT FAR...

URP... THIS SUCKS. I FEEL SICK JUST LOOKING AT THE DAMN THING.

CRAP. FOR ME, TAXIS ARE JUST AS BAD AS TOUR BUSES. AND THAT WEIRD SMELL THEY ALWAYS HAVE— IT HAS THE DESTRUCTIVE POWER TO LAY ME FLAT ALMOST INSTANTLY.

IF ANYONE EVER FINDS OUT I GET CARSICK, THIS REPUTATION I'VE BUILT UP WILL CRUMBLE TO THE GROUND. I MIGHT NOT EVEN BE ABLE TO GO OUT IN PUBLIC.

COME ON, TAKENOUCHI! WE CAN'T DO IT WITHOUT YOU!

I KNOW WE'RE IN A HURRY, BUT IF WE GO TO BASS AND THEY'RE READY FOR US, WE'LL REALLY BE IN FOR IT. I THINK WE SHOULD GO BACK INSIDE AND THINK THINGS OUT CLEARLY.

BEFORE WE GET IN, LET ME SAY SOMETHIN'!

RIGHT! IT'S **DEFINITELY** A TRAP! SO FIRST, WE SHOULD COME UP WITH A PLAN.

I'm lucky they're so dumb!

YOU'RE RIGHT. IT COULD BE A **TRAP** TO LURE US OUT INTO THE OPEN. MAYBE WE **SHOULD** HAMMER OUT A GOOD PLAN FIRST!

vwsh

ALL RIGHT! THEN WE'LL FORMULATE OUR STRATEGY ON THE WAY!

AND IN THE **MIDDLE**. WHAT THE HELL?!

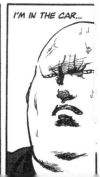

I'M IN THE CAR...

AND, WHO'S THAT BASTARD IN THE PASSENGER SEAT? HE LOOKS LIKE SOME KINDA **ROCK SINGER**.

NOW I CAN'T EVEN GET ANY FRESH AIR FROM THE WINDOW. OR JUMP OUT IF I NEED TO!

HUH? BUT, WHY?

S-STOP THE CAR...

CRAP. JUST THINKING ABOUT ALL THAT MADE ME FEEL SICKER. I HAVE TO CONCENTRATE...

I'M NOT SURE I UNDERSTAND.

I CAN'T LET YOU TWO GET TANGLED UP IN THIS.

WHY? WELL, UH...

HOW CAN YOU SAY THAT? WE **MUST** STICK TOGETHER!

LOOK, I'M GONNA WALK OVER THERE ON MY... HEY, LEGGO!

I THOUGHT YOU SAID THEY WERE PANSIES.

THE GUYS AT BASS ARE **REALLY** TOUGH. THERE'S GONNA BE A LOT OF BLOOD SPILLED IF WE GO THERE.

I ONLY RECENTLY CAME TO TOKYO, SO I'M AFRAID I DON'T KNOW THE ROADS AROUND HERE...

YES?

EXCUSE ME, SIR?

I'M GONNA BE DEAD BEFORE WE GET THERE.

EVEN IF WE DIE, WE DIE **TOGETHER!** I CANNOT LET YOU GET OUT OF THIS CAB!

WELL IF HE DOESN'T KNOW THE WAY, HE DOESN'T KNOW THE WAY.

I THOUGHT YOU SAID THERE'S NO TIME TO LOSE!

THAT'S ALL RIGHT. EVEN IF WE HAVE TO TAKE A DETOUR, WE...

· · ·

TAKENOUCHI, RELAX! THAT'S NOT THE DRIVER!

TO HELL WITH THAT! IF YOU TRY TAKING ANY FRICKIN' DETOURS, I'LL FRICKIN' MURDER YA!

I SHOULDN'T HAVE SAID THAT... IF I LOOK AT THE MAP TOO LONG, IT MIGHT MAKE ME FEEL EVEN *SICKER*. I BETTER FIND THE SHORTEST ROUTE AS FAST AS I CAN!

SURE!

GIMME THE MAP! I'LL FIGURE OUT WHERE WE'RE GOIN'!!

世界地図
WORLD MAP

HUH?

WE HEAD SOUTH FROM THE SCANDINAVIAN PENINSULA, PASS OVER THE PANAMA CANAL, THEN CROSS THE INTERNATIONAL DATELINE, AND...

HMM, WE SHOULD BE RIGHT ABOUT **HERE**, SO...

BWAP

THIS IS A FRICKIN' **WORLD MAP**, YOU MORON!

WILL THEY BE ABLE TO RESCUE MAEDA?!

OH, CRAP! TAKEN-OUCHI PASSED OUT AGAIN!

AH, YOU'RE RIGHT! WHAT'S MORE, IT HAS RUSSIA LISTED AS THE SOVIET UNION!

世界地図
WORLD MAP
1981 年度版
EDITION

A FIRST FOR CROMARTIE—
TO BE CONTINUED IN THE SECOND PART!!

CHAPTER TEN: **TAXI 2**

WASTING NO TIME, THE MEN HAVE TAKEN A TAXI, ONLY TO FIND THE DRIVER DOES NOT KNOW THE LOCAL ROADS. THE ATMOSPHERE INSIDE THE CRISIS-STRICKEN CAB IS HEAVY INDEED.

IT HAS BEEN 2 HOURS SINCE MAEDA WAS ABDUCTED BY BASS HIGH SCHOOL.

IF I'D KNOWN THIS WAS GONNA HAPPEN, I WOULD'VE EATEN SOMETHING MORE **DIGESTIBLE** FOR LUNCH.

IT'S TOO LATE TO TELL 'EM I HATE RIDING IN CARS.

AND TAKENOUCHI'S MOTION SICKNESS HAS REACHED ITS PEAK.

I DON'T KNOW ANYTHING ABOUT THIS "MAEDA" GUY. ONLY THAT WE'RE IN THE SAME CLASS... I THINK I'M GONNA PUKE. LET ME OUTTA THE DAMN CAB!

WHY DO I HAVE TO DEAL WITH THIS CRAP, ANYWAY?

I'M SORRY. IT SEEMS WE'VE MADE A STRATEGIC ERROR.

WE COULDA **WALKED** THERE IN **20** MINUTES!

LOOKS LIKE WE'VE BEEN IN THIS TAXI FOR OVER AN HOUR NOW.

YES! THAT'S RIGHT! WE DON'T HAVE ANY MONEY ON US, SO WE BETTER GET OUT QUICK!

AT THIS RATE, THE FARE WILL BE OUT-RAGEOUS.

YEAH! HECK, WE COULD RIDE ALL DAY IF WE WANT!

SO WE CAN AFFORD THE FARE, RIGHT, HAYASHIDA-KUN?

HEY, DON'T WORRY! I WON 120,000* YEN AT THE PACHINKO PARLOR YESTERDAY!

*ABOUT $ 1,100 US

LISTENING TO YOU TWO IS PISSIN' ME OFF! SO SHUT THE HELL UP!!

SORRY. I DIDN'T...

WHAT THE HELL DO YOU THINK WE'RE DOING-- RESCUING OUR FRIEND OR TAKING A JOYRIDE?!

vroom

HUH?

DON'T JUST SIT THERE ALL QUIET. SAY SOMETHIN'!

CRAP, IT'S TOO QUIET. NOW I FEEL EVEN SICKER...

FINE. BUT YOU CAN'T JUST TALK ABOUT **ANYTHING**.

I DON'T REALLY GET IT, BUT OKAY, LET'S TALK.

SHUT YER HOLE! I CHANGED MY MIND, SO START **TALKIN'** ABOUT SOMETHING!

BUT YOU JUST TOLD US TO BE QUIET.

THEN WHAT **SHOULD** WE TALK ABOUT?

IF YOU GO TALKING ABOUT THAT KINDA STUFF BEFORE A BRAWL, IT KILLS THE TENSION.

I DON'T WANT TO HEAR ABOUT ANY NASTY SHIT. OR ABOUT HOW IT'S HOT OUT, OR HOW YOU FEEL TIRED. NOTHING **NEGATIVE**.

AND ANOTHER THING! REMEMBER, YOU'RE NOT JUST TALKING TO EACH OTHER. YOU GOTTA LET **ME** IN ON THE CONVERSATION, TOO.

BUT WOULDN'T THAT **LOWER** THE TENSION EVEN MORE?

I GUESS YOU COULD TALK ABOUT, SAY, THE GENTLE BREEZE THAT BLOWS SOFTLY ACROSS THE PLAINS. SOMETHIN' LIKE THAT'D BE BEST.

YOU HAVEN'T EVEN TRIED!

SORRY. I CAN'T DO IT.

: : :

YOU GOT IT? NOW START TALKING, BUT DON'T FORGET WHAT I JUST TOLD YOU!

WE... WE'RE OUT IN THE MOUN-TAINS!

I DON'T RECOGNIZE THIS PLACE AT ALL!

vroom

LOOK OUT THE WINDOW!

OH... OH MY GOD!

I'M STARTING TO WORRY LESS ABOUT MAEDA AND MORE ABOUT US!

WHAT ARE WE GOING TO DO NOW?

Country roads sure are bumpy...

I KNOW YOU'RE NOT FAMILIAR WITH THE ROADS, BUT THIS IS TOO MUCH!

I'M SORRY. IT APPEARS WE'VE SOMEHOW ENDED UP NEAR MY PARENTS' HOME.

: : :

LOOK! FREDDIE IS READING THE MAP!

世界地図
WORLD MAP

!!

I GET IT! IT'S SOME KIND OF ANIMAL INSTINCT!

HE'S POINTING RIGHT. DOES HE ACTUALLY KNOW THE WAY?

fwp

YES, SIR!

TAKE THE NEXT LEFT!

fwip

YES, SIR!

PLEASE TAKE A RIGHT, CABBIE!

screek

IT'S BEEN A LONG TRIP, BUT ONLY A LITTLE FARTHER, THEN I'LL TAKE THIS ANGER OUT ON THOSE BASS GUYS!

Damn, I feel bad!

WE'RE DEFINITELY GETTING CLOSER NOW!

IS IT JUST ME, OR ARE WE ACTUALLY GETTING **CLOSER?**

PUT THE FEAR OF CROMARTIE IN 'EM! WE'LL WIPE THOSE BASTARDS OUT!

HELL YEAH!

ALL RIGHT! LET'S DO IT!

WE MADE IT!

THIS IS OUR OWN FRICKIN' SCHOOL!

CROMARTIE HIGH SCH

SCRASH

WE'RE BACK WHERE WE STARTED...

WHERE IS EVERY-ONE?

The Bass guys went home.

← MAEDA

THAT DRIVER WAS THE BADDEST DUDE OF ALL.

 ICHIRO YAMAMOTO

Introduced in the first chapter, he was a close friend of Kamiyama. His motto is, "A scholar and an athlete." He instilled within Kamiyama the courage to stand his ground against bullies and not run away. He would have had an important role in the story, but ended up only appearing in the first chapter. So completely was this character forgotten that the author himself at one point asked his editor, "Uh, who was that guy? You know, the dude who was in the first chapter!" Perhaps the careless treatment of this character is a result of the uninspired name he was given. There's probably no point in even making a character introduction for him. It's entirely possible that even Kamiyama has already forgotten about him. At any rate, even I am not sure what to think about this Cromartie reject.

KEN HIRAI

Introduced in the fifth chapter, this 17-year-old ought to be an 11th grader, but after failing his 1st year classes, he now must repeat the 10th grade. His fighting abilities are unknown, but because of his age difference, he's already in a class of his own. It just goes to show how much age can impact one's social standing in high school. It might also explain why he is so preachy. The advice he imparts upon Kamiyama might seem sensible enough at first, but it's actually pretty meaningless. He has no particular forte, so people gave him the amusing nickname, Hirai The Flunker. Since he is estranged from the rest of the class and has nobody to talk to, conversations with him may take a very long time. His motto is, "Everyone puts on their trousers one leg at a time." How could you flunk a grade at a school like Cromartie?!

FREDDIE ➡

Cromartie High School's mystery figure. He has a hairy chest. Beyond this, details such as his real name, age, and country of origin are unknown (LOL). However, we *do* know his blood type is B. Whether or not he is even a student remains a mystery. It certainly is difficult to eliminate the possibility he's just some old guy wandering around the school. From the first time he appeared, he has said absolutely nothing, and for some reason he has become attached to Kamiyama. Freddie is always lightly dressed, especially his upper body. He is feared throughout the school, though not in the sense that the other badasses are. Naturally, his motto is, "Rock you."

⬅ YUTAKA TAKENOUCHI

The underground kingpin of Cromartie High's 1st year class. (What is an "underground kingpin" anyway?) Takenouchi loves to travel, but hates being in vehicles. His strength is enough to make his longtime enemies at Bass High School tremble; in terms of respect, he has no equal. If only he didn't get motion sickness so easily, he would have made a perfectly fine main character. This single drawback is most regrettable. Takenouchi has come to fear Kamiyama because whenever the two are together, he ends up in some sort of unpleasant situation. Takenouchi has a cute, shaved head. His grandeur, which is far beyond that of a normal 16-year-old, has attracted many female fans. (Seriously!) His motto is, "Stick with your New Years resolutions."

SUCH THINGS ARE **ILLUSIONS**, OFTEN THE PRODUCTS OF OVERACTIVE IMAGINATIONS, AND THEY CAN BE EXPLAINED **SCIENTIFICALLY**.

I SIMPLY DO NOT BELIEVE IN "PARANORMAL PHENOMENA" LIKE THAT.

THERE IS A DEVIL AT CROMARTIE HIGH...

LOOK, ARGUING WILL GET US NOWHERE. WHY DON'T WE JUST GO HAVE A LOOK FOR OURSELVES?

THEN WHAT **ARE** YOU TALKING ABOUT?

YEAH, BUT WHAT I'M TALKING ABOUT AIN'T LIKE THAT!

RATTLE

ONE, TWO...

OKAY, LET'S GO.

SEE?

EVERYONE KNOWS THAT BADASSES FROM ALL OVER JAPAN COME TO CROMARTIE, BUT **THIS**, WELL...

I DON'T THINK THIS IS A PROBLEM FOR **SCIENCE**...

THERE ARE MANY THINGS SCIENCE HAS YET TO EXPLAIN.

CROMARTIE MAY BE CONSIDERED A **SCHOOL FOR IDIOTS**, BUT I CAN'T IMAGINE THEY'D ADMIT ANIMALS. DOES THIS MEAN WE'RE SUPPOSED TO CONSIDER HIM A HUMAN?

HE AIN'T BAD AT ALL! HE'S NOT EVEN **HUMAN**!

I CAN'T BELIEVE SOMEONE **THIS** BAD WOULD...

WHAT COULD POSSIBLY MAKE YOU THINK **HE** IS A HUMAN?!

THE HELL THERE IS!

SURE ENOUGH! THERE'S ONE IN EVERY CLASS, RIGHT?

THERE **ARE** SOME PRETTY HAIRY PEOPLE...

NO, I'M SORRY. HAVING A WRISTWATCH ISN'T ENOUGH TO CONVINCE ME THAT SOMETHING IS A HUMAN.

YIKES! YOU'RE RIGHT!

WELL, HE **IS** WEARING A WATCH...

W H A T ? !

WOW... HE'S MAKING A CALL.

HOW'D HE KNOW THE NUMBER?

DON'T TELL ME YOU'RE ON THE PHONE WITH THE GORILLA!

: : :

LOOK, FREDDIE IS, TOO!

: : :

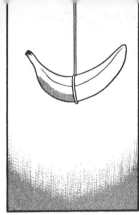

THERE'S NO MAKIN' YOU HAPPY.

NO WAY! EVEN A GORILLA COULD USE A PHONE!

HE'S WEARING A WRISTWATCH AND USING A PHONE. ISN'T THAT ENOUGH FOR US TO CONSIDER HIM HUMAN?

IT'S SOMETHING I SAW ON TV ONCE. AMERICAN RESEARCHERS USED THIS SETUP TO TEST A CHIMPANZEE'S INTELLIGENCE. IF HE CAN USE THOSE TOOLS TO GET AT THE BANANA, IT PROVES HE'S AT LEAST SMARTER THAN A CHIMP.

WHAT'S THE DEAL, KAMIYAMA?

A BOX, A STICK, AND A BANANA?

KAMIYAMA! START THE TEST NOW!

I GOTCHA! SO... HOW DOES HE GET THE BANANA?

EXACTLY.

THEN IF HE CAN GET THE BANANA, YOU'LL RECOGNIZE HIM AS A HUMAN?

FINE. GO AHEAD, FREDDIE-- GET THAT BANANA!

BUT **FREDDIE** WANTS THE BANANA!

STOP, FREDDIE! THAT'S ENOUGH!

RARGH

OKAY, SO ANYWAY... WE TREAT HIM LIKE A HUMAN IF HE'S ABLE TO GET THE BANANA, HUH?

Freddie couldn't do it...

HUH? OH, SO **THAT'S** HOW!

ALL HE HAD TO DO WAS GET ON THE BOX AND USE THE STICK. HOW COULD THIS HAPPEN?

IF THAT'S HOW IT'S GOING TO BE, TRY TO GET IT.

GOOD. NOW WE'LL KNOW FOR SURE WHETHER HE'S HUMAN OR GORILLA!

OOGA. OOGA.

HEY, THERE HE IS!

*Kanji = Chinese characters

CHAPTER TWELVE: **NORMAL DE GO**!

WONDER IF IT'S 'CUZ WE'RE ALWAYS HANGIN' AROUND...

'CUZ THE COFFEE SUCKS HERE!

THIS PLACE NEVER GETS CUSTOMERS.

YEAH. MORE LIKE YOU'D BE **GETTIN'** HIT!

AIN'T NO WAY YOU'D EVER SCORE, SO SHADDUP!

SO THE OTHER DAY, I WAS ALL HITTIN' ON THIS HOT CHICK, AND...

YEAH. YOU GOT LIKE, NO CREDIBILITY.

YOU'RE JUST A PUNK YOURSELF, SO SHADDUP!

LAST NIGHT, I WAS MESSIN' WITH SOME PUNKS, AND...

BUT IF YA KEEP TALKIN' ABOUT THE SAME OLD STUFF DAY IN AND DAY OUT, IT'S GONNA GET BORING. YEAH, WE'RE BADASSES, BUT IT DOESN'T MEAN WE **ALWAYS** GOTTA TALK ABOUT THAT KINDA STUFF.

WE ALWAYS HANG AROUND HERE, AND WE'RE ALWAYS TALKIN' ABOUT FIGHTIN' AND MOTORCYCLES AND WOMEN AND **PORNO** AND STUFF, RIGHT?

WE COULD EVEN TALK ABOUT HEALTH AND STUFF.

HEY, YEAH! I MEAN, SOCIETY'S ALWAYS LOOKIN' DOWN ON US, RIGHT?

I'M THINKIN', WHY NOT TALK ABOUT SOCIETY AND CRAP, TOO, YA KNOW?

HEY... YOU'RE PRETTY SMART!

DAMN, THAT'S RIGHT!

WE AIN'T NORMAL, SO HOW CAN WE TALK ABOUT NORMAL STUFF?

WHOA, HOLD ON A SEC.

WHEN THE HECK DID YOU GET HERE?!

OH YEAH! KAMIYAMA!

SLRP

NO, WAIT-- THERE IS ONE NORMAL DUDE!

AHEM...

FEAR NOT, MY FRIENDS. WHEN IT COMES TO NORMAL CONVERSATIONS, I HAVE NO EQUAL.

CAN YA HELP US OUT?

SO, HOW WAS IT?

PIKE! WELL, THIS IS THE SEASON.

SPEAKING OF FALL, I GRILLED SOME PIKE YESTER-DAY.

DAMN, NOW THAT IS NORMAL!

HOLY CRAP!

MAYBE SOMETHING ALONG THE LINES OF "IT'S GOTTEN RATHER CHILLY LATELY. LOOKS LIKE FALL IS ON ITS WAY." RIGHT?

WELL, IT **DID** TASTE GOOD, BUT IT WAS NOTHING LIKE ON THE COOKING SHOWS, WHERE PEOPLE EAT IT, AND SAY...

WHADDYA MEAN "ALL RIGHT"? AUTUMN PIKE'S GOT ALL THE FAT, SO IT SHOULD BE, LIKE, DELICIOUS!

HMM. WELL, I SUPPOSE IT WAS **ALL RIGHT**...

YEAH, I SEE YOUR POINT. THEY DO TEND TO **EXAGGER-ATE** THINGS ON TV.

IT WAS GOOD, BUT NOT **THAT** GOOD.

OH MY GOD, THIS IS AMAZING!!

WHEREAS IN REALITY, THINGS LIKE THAT ARE QUITE RARE! IT'S TRUE PIKE IS DELICIOUS, BUT IT WASN'T THE FIRST TIME IN MY LIFE I'VE EATEN IT. AND BESIDES, I FORGOT THE GRATED RADISH...

IF WE WATCH TOO MUCH TV OR READ TOO MANY **MANGA**, WE MAY END UP WITH UNREALISTIC EXPECTATIONS, HOPES AND IDEALS.

WHOA! **ANOTHER** NORMAL CONVER-SATION!

THE AUTUMN BREEZE FELT RATHER INVITING THE OTHER DAY, SO I WENT OUT FOR A STROLL.

THIS IS A NORMAL CONVER-SATION, MORE OR LESS.

WHAT HAPPENED THEN?

AFTER I HELPED HER UP, SHE OFFERED TO TREAT ME TO A CUP OF TEA.

I HAPPENED UPON AN OLD WOMAN, WHO HAD COLLAPSED ON A CROSSWALK.

WHAT HAPPENED NEXT?!

WHOA, WHAT?!

WELL, IMAGINE MY SURPRISE WHEN I FOUND OUT SHE BELONGED TO A VERY WEALTHY FAMILY.

DON'T BE **SILLY**. WHY WOULD SHE REWARD ME JUST FOR HELPING HER UP OFF THE CROSSWALK? IF IT WERE A TV SHOW OR A NOVEL, THEN MAYBE THE STORY WOULD HAVE DEVELOPED INTO SOMETHING...

WHAT THE HELL?! SHE SHOULD HAVE GIVEN YA LIKE 100 MILLION YEN* OR SOMETHIN'!

NOTHING REALLY. I DRANK MY TEA, AND WENT HOME.

* About $900,000

WHAT, **ANOTHER** NORMAL STORY?!

SO I WAS GOING INTO TOWN, AND...

GET A GRIP! WE'RE TALKIN' **NORMAL**, REMEMBER?

ARRGH! THIS MAKES ME WANNA GO ON A RAMPAGE!

BUT THIS IS A **NORMAL** STORY, AFTER ALL.

THIS TIME, I HAPPENED UPON A MIDDLE-AGED BUSINESSMAN WHO HAD COLLAPSED ON A CROSSWALK.

AFTER I HELPED HIM UP, HE OFFERED TO TREAT ME TO A CUP OF TEA.

SO YOU DRANK YOUR TEA, AND WENT HOME AGAIN, RIGHT? DON'T TELL US THE SAME DAMN STORY TWICE! MAN, I'M GONNA KILL YOU!

TRYIN' TO TRICK US WITH ONE OF YOUR LITTLE TEASERS, HUH? WELL, YOU WON'T FOOL US AGAIN! NOT WITH YOUR STUPID **NORMAL** STORIES...

IT TURNED OUT THE MAN WAS REALLY AN ALIEN, AND IN RETURN FOR HELPING HIM, HE OFFERED TO TAKE ME FOR A RIDE IN HIS **UFO**.

WHOA, REALLY?!

JUST LISTEN. THIS STORY DOESN'T END THE SAME WAY.

HOLY CRAP! SO YOU RODE IN A UFO?!

WHOA... THIS AIN'T NO **NORMAL** STORY!!

NO, IT WAS AN ADAMSKI TYPE.

WAS IT A CIGAR-SHAPED UFO?!

UFO?!

· · · · ·

WELL, ACTUALLY...

HE **LOST** HIS KEYS TO THE UFO. WE COULDN'T EVEN GET IN!

I GUESS IT TURNED OUT TO BE A NORMAL STORY AFTER ALL, HUH?

AH, FOR CHRISSAKE! SO YOU DIDN'T GET TO RIDE IT?

UH, I DON'T THINK IT SOUNDS VERY NORMAL.

SHOULD'VE CALLED THE AAA.

CHAPTER THIRTEEN: **AMBITIONS FOR EMPIRE**

BY MEANS OF HIS FATHER'S POLITICAL MIGHT, AS WELL AS HIS OWN BRUTE STRENGTH, TAKESHI HAS COME TO CONTROL 18 DIFFERENT SCHOOLS. HOPING TO SINK HIS VENOMOUS FANGS INTO NEW PREY, HE HAS TRANSFERRED TO THE SCHOOL KNOWN AS THE LOWEST OF THE LOW—CROMARTIE.

TAKESHI HOKUTO (16) SON OF THE HOKUTO FAMILY, HEIR TO THE HOKUTO FOUNDATION. HIS FATHER IS CHAIRMAN OF THE HOKUTO GROUP, AS WELL AS CROMARTIE HIGH SCHOOL'S ADMINISTRATIVE DIRECTOR.

Henchman

IF ANYONE TRIES TO OPPOSE YOU, WE'LL USE YOUR FATHER'S AUTHORITY, AND HAVE 'EM **EXPELLED**. NO NEED TO DIRTY OUR OWN HANDS.

HEH HEH.

SO THIS FILTHY HOLE IS CROMARTIE, EH?

I WILL DRIVE MY **IDEALS** INTO THESE INCOMPETENT PIGS AND **RULE** OVER THEM ALL.

TOO BAD IF YOU HAVE TO DO THAT ON YOUR FIRST DAY, THOUGH. AND TOO BAD FOR THEM!

I COULD EVEN HAVE THE **TEACHERS** FIRED, IF I WANT.

RATTLE

YES, SIR.

HEH. I CAN TAKE CARE OF THIS ALONE. WAIT HERE. I'LL SHOW THESE PIGS WHO THEY'RE DEALING WITH.

1-1

AND I'LL START HERE.

RATTLE カラララ...

P-CHK

NO, THIS WAS SOMETHING BEYOND A MERE BADASS OR DELINQUENT!

WELL, THIS SCHOOL **IS** FAMOUS FOR ITS BADASSES.

I THOUGHT I SAW A **PRO WRESTLER** JUST NOW. MY EYES MUST BE PLAYING TRICKS ON ME.

WHAT HAPPENED? YOU LOOK PALE...

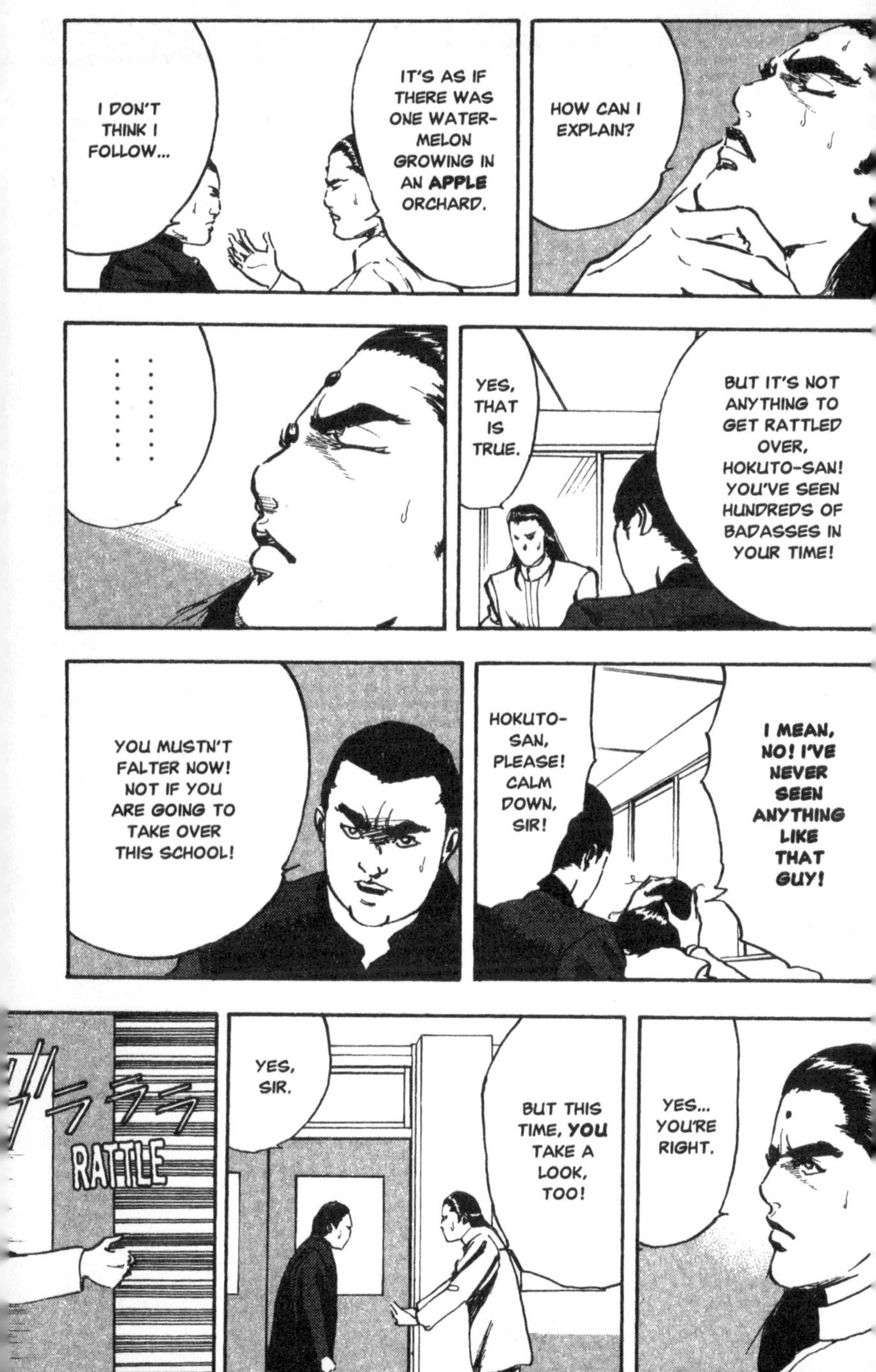

HOW CAN I EXPLAIN?
IT'S AS IF THERE WAS ONE WATER-MELON GROWING IN AN **APPLE** ORCHARD.
I DON'T THINK I FOLLOW...
BUT IT'S NOT ANYTHING TO GET RATTLED OVER, HOKUTO-SAN! YOU'VE SEEN HUNDREDS OF BADASSES IN YOUR TIME!
YES, THAT IS TRUE.
......
I MEAN, NO! I'VE NEVER SEEN ANYTHING LIKE THAT GUY!
HOKUTO-SAN, PLEASE! CALM DOWN, SIR!
YOU MUSTN'T FALTER NOW! NOT IF YOU ARE GOING TO TAKE OVER THIS SCHOOL!
YES... YOU'RE RIGHT.
BUT THIS TIME, **YOU** TAKE A LOOK, TOO!
YES, SIR.
RATTLE

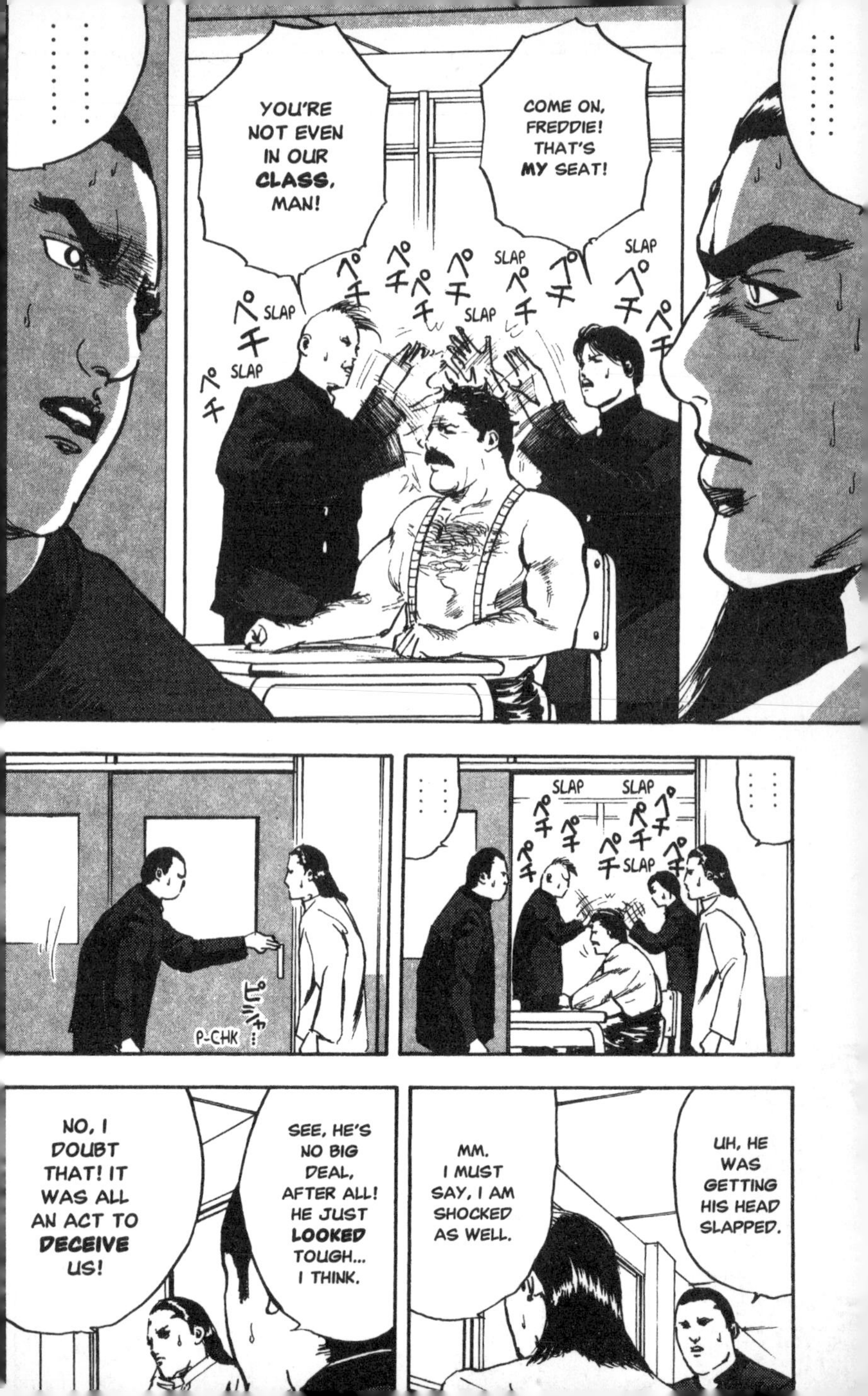
.....
.....
COME ON, FREDDIE! THAT'S MY SEAT!
YOU'RE NOT EVEN IN OUR CLASS, MAN!
SLAP
SLAP
SLAP
SLAP
SLAP
ペチ ペチ ペチ ペチ ペチ ペチ ペチ ペチ ペチ ペチ
....
....
SLAP
SLAP
SLAP
ペチ ペチ ペチ ペチ ペチ ペチ
P-CHK
ピシャ…
UH, HE WAS GETTING HIS HEAD SLAPPED.
MM. I MUST SAY, I AM SHOCKED AS WELL.
SEE, HE'S NO BIG DEAL, AFTER ALL! HE JUST LOOKED TOUGH... I THINK.
NO, I DOUBT THAT! IT WAS ALL AN ACT TO DECEIVE US!

: : :
: : :

STILL NO PROBLEM! IF THE GUY EVER GIVES YA GRIEF, JUST HAVE HIM **EXPELLED!**

I HEARD THEY DON'T SCREEN THEIR APPLICANTS HERE.

HOW DID A GUY LIKE THAT EVEN GET INTO THIS SCHOOL?

YOU WORRY TOO MUCH.

BUT IF I DO THAT, HE MIGHT TRY TO GET REVENGE.

PLEASE CALM DOWN. EVEN IF HE DOES LOOK LIKE A MONSTER, HE'S JUST ANOTHER **PERSON.** IF YOU LOOK AT IT THAT WAY, THERE'S NOTHING TO BE ALARMED ABOUT!

THEN THERE'S NOTHING WE CAN DO!

BESIDES, I GET THE FEELING THAT GUY'LL KEEP COMING, EVEN IF HE'S EXPELLED.

ラララ
RATTLE

OKAY. LET'S DO IT!

HAVE SOME CONFIDENCE, BOSS! LET'S OPEN THE DOOR!

TOO TRUE. HE **IS** ONLY HUMAN, AFTER ALL.

p-chk

HELLO, MOMMY?! I CAN'T GO INTO THE CLASSROOM. PUT DADDY ON!

NOW **THAT** GUY AIN'T HUMAN!

NOT PIGS, BUT GORILLAS.

I AM THE **CHOSEN ONE**. TO FULLFILL MY IDEALS, I HAVE TAKEN OVER MANY HIGH SCHOOLS, AND I WILL MAKE CROMARTIE MINE AS WELL. "DEFEAT" IS NOT A WORD IN MY DICTIONARY.

MY NAME IS TAKESHI HOKUTO. I AM THE SON OF CROMARTIE HIGH SCHOOL'S ADMINISTRATIVE DIRECTOR. I AM RATHER BRILLIANT, IF I DO SAY SO MYSELF, AND I HAVE NEVER BEEN DEFEATED IN A FIGHT.

WHAT?

WELL, ACTUALLY, THERE'S MORE TO IT THAN THAT.

THE GORILLA GOT THE BEST OF US EARLIER. WE SHOULD AIM TO **SUPPRESS** THOSE THREE.

TAKENOUCHI, FREDDIE, AND THAT GORILLA... THESE GUYS (WELL, TWO GUYS AND ONE BEAST) ARE RUNNING THINGS IN THE 1ST YEAR CLASS.

I SEE. THEN THAT'S WHO I NEED TO TAKE OUT. WHOEVER HE IS, HE STANDS NO CHANCE AGAINST **ME**.

ACCORDING TO MY INFORMATION, THESE THREE OPERATE UNDER THE COMMAND OF **ANOTHER INDIVIDUAL**.

THE ONE YOU'RE AFTER IS...

I CAN'T WASTE ANY TIME IN DOMINATING THESE PIGS. WHO EXACTLY IS THIS GUY?

HM? CAN I HELP YOU?

THIS GUY.

Oh, boy. One more wacko...

LISTEN, AND LISTEN WELL! MY NAME IS TAKESHI HOKUTO. MY IDEALS DEMAND I TAKE OVER THIS SCHOOL!

NOW JUST A MOMENT! WHAT ON EARTH ARE YOU TALKING ABOUT?

BUT YOU'RE JUST AN INSIGNIFICANT **PEON!** GROVEL BEFORE ME, WORM!

HEH... DON'T YOU FOOLS UNDERSTAND? MY FATHER IS THIS SCHOOL'S **DIRECTOR.** HE COULD HAVE ALL OF YOU EXPELLED ON A WHIM!

WHO DO YOU THINK YOU ARE? WHAT GIVES YOU THE RIGHT TO SPEAK SO VIOLENTLY?!

I'LL START BY ELIMINATING **YOU!**

THIS IS A **PUBLIC** SCHOOL, DUDE. WE DON'T HAVE ANY DIRECTOR!

EH? WHAT DO YOU WANT, MOHAWK?

HEY, CAN I SAY SOMETHIN'?

AND CHECK OUT YOUR UNIFORM--IT AIN'T ANYTHING LIKE OURS. IT'S, LIKE, **WHITE!**

WHAT? **PUBLIC?**

HE'S RIGHT!

AND I CAN'T EVEN USE MY FATHER'S POLITICAL INFLUENCE AT THIS SCHOOL.

NOW WHAT DO I DO? I'VE ALREADY COMPLETED THE TRANSFER PROCEDURES. IF I ADMIT I MADE A MISTAKE NOW, I'LL NEVER OUTLIVE THE SHAME.

I'VE COME TO THE **WRONG** SCHOOL.

SO BE IT! I ACCEPT THIS CHALLENGE. I'LL MANAGE, EVEN IF I NEED TO *LIE* MY WAY OUT!

YOU O.K.?

BUT I CAN'T BACK OUT NOW, AFTER SAYING ALL THAT!

WHAT IS WITH THIS GUY?

HUH?

MY FATHER IS **NOT** THE ADMINISTRATIVE DIRECTOR OF THIS SCHOOL!

ALL RIGHT. LISTEN UP, YOU CRETINS!

THE ONE WHO'S REALLY PULLING THE STRINGS IN THE JAPANESE GOVERNMENT-- THE **DARK PRIME MINISTER!**

FLASH

NOW HOLD ON A SECOND. MY FATHER IS...

BUT **YOU'RE** THE ONE WHO SAID HE IS.

THEN WHAT'S THE BIG DEAL, YA NUT?

NOT EVEN A LITTLE KID WOULD BUY THAT NONSENSE!

NOW HE'S DONE IT! WHAT THE HELL IS HE SAYING?

YES! CONTROLLING A MERE PUBLIC HIGH SCHOOL IS A **TRIFLE** TO HIM. YOU ARE NOTHING BUT PAWNS AT HIS COMMAND!

PULLING THE STRINGS?

THEY BELIEVE HIM! THESE GUYS ARE SO FRICKIN' DUMB!!

UH... YEAH.

HOLY CRAP!

WHOA! ARE YOU SERIOUS?!

YOU'RE EXACTLY RIGHT... PERHAPS.

I ALWAYS THOUGHT THERE WAS SOMETHING FUNNY GOIN' ON HERE.

SO DOES THAT MEAN WE ARE EVIL MINIONS, TOO?

JUST BETWEEN US, THIS SCHOOL WAS ESTABLISHED TO HELP TRAIN THE EVIL MINIONS OF THE DARK PRIME MINISTER. SPEAK NOT A WORD OF THIS TO ANYONE, UNDERSTAND?

SON OF... YOU MEAN ME?! EH, WELL I...

Oh, son of darkness...

SO, WHAT BRINGS A SON OF EVIL LIKE YOURSELF HERE?

EVEN I DON'T KNOW WHAT I'M TALKING ABOUT ANYMORE. I HAVE TO PULL THIS STORY TOGETHER.

THERE ARE TIMES WHEN A MAN MUST FIGHT FOR JUSTICE, EVEN IF IT MEANS GOING AGAINST HIS OWN FATHER. IT IS A DIFFICULT PATH, BUT...

AH! YES, THAT'S RIGHT! UH, IT'S LIKE THIS...

STRING-PULLER? YOU MEAN YOUR FATHER?

I HAVE SET OUT TO OVER-THROW THAT CONNIVING STRING-PULLER!

A... ARE YOU SERIOUS?

WILL YOU LET US HELP YOU! PLEASE! FOR GREAT JUSTICE!

CLENCH

CRAP. DID THEY FINALLY FIGURE IT OUT?

HUH?

CAN I ASK YOU SOMETHING?

FROM THIS DAY FORTH, WE ARE ALLIES OF JUSTICE!

VERY WELL, THEN. THE CAST IS ASSEMBLED.

DON'T BE A FOOL! WHY, YOU'RE ONE OF US!

NOW JUST A DARN MINUTE. DON'T YOU GO LEAVIN' ME OUT!

YEAH!!

ALL RIGHT! STARTING TOMORROW, LET'S DO THE BEST WE CAN!

WHAT AM I SUPPOSED TO DO NOW?

YEAH, YOU DID THAT, GENIUS.

CHAPTER FIFTEEN: **HOKUTO'S ASSASSINATION PLOT**

TAKESHI HOKUTO (16)
IN A CURIOUS AND UNPRECEDENTEDLY HAM-FISTED MOVE, HE TRANSFERRED TO CROMARTIE HIGH SCHOOL BY MISTAKE. (HE IS SUPPOSEDLY THE SON OF ANOTHER SCHOOL'S ADMINI-STRATIVE DIRECTOR.)

FEARFUL THAT THIS DISGRACE MIGHT RUIN HIM—ESPECIALLY AFTER AN EXCEEDINGLY SHOCKING DEBUT—HE ATTEMPTED TO HIDE HIS BLUNDER BY PAINTING A PICTURE OF LIES AND INTRIGUE. HOWEVER, THE SUBTERFUGE ONLY MADE HIS PREDICAMENT WORSE.

There's no such thing as a Dark Prime Minister!

BUT ACCORDING TO YOUR STORY, WE HAVE TO TEAM UP WITH THEM AND BATTLE AGAINST THE DARK PRIME MINISTER AND HIS NEFARIOUS SCHEMES.

ENOUGH! IT'S TOO EMBARRAS-SING TO EVEN **THINK** I SAID SOMETHING LIKE THAT!

YOU **DID** SAY YOUR FATHER IS AN EVIL MANIPU-LATOR.

I'LL BET THEY'RE PLAYING THEIR TIME AWAY AT THE ARCADE RIGHT NOW.

WELL, THEY SURE ARE DUMB...

WE NEED TO CALM DOWN AND THINK THIS OUT. HMM, IF THEY'RE STUPID ENOUGH TO TAKE MY STORY SERIOUSLY, THEN I'M SURE THEY'LL HAVE FORGOTTEN ABOUT IT COMPLETELY IN A DAY OR TWO.

THEY HAVE GOOD MEMORIES FOR A BUNCH OF MINDLESS BUFFOONS!

CA... CAPTAIN?!

CAPTAIN!

SALUTE THE CAPTAIN!

WE'VE BEEN LOOKING FOR YOU, SIR!

THEY MUST HAVE THE WRONG IDEA, CAPT-- I MEAN, HOKUTO-SAN.

WHERE DID YOU GET THOSE OUTFITS?!

BUT WHY, CAPTAIN, SIR?

SHHH!

DON'T CALL ME THAT IN FRONT OF OTHER PEOPLE!

GOD, THIS IS SO HUMILI-ATING!

WHAT THE HELL...

CAPTAIN?

THE REASON BEING...

LOOK, WE NEED TO KEEP A **LOW PROFILE**!

CRAP! THEY'RE SERIOUS. I HAVE TO DO SOMETHING...

WHAT, DO WE STAND OUT?

I'M SORRY, SIR. HOW CARELESS OF US!

THIS IS A HIGHLY **CLASSIFIED MISSION**! UNDERSTAND?

THAT'S RIGHT... I WAS SO BUSY TRYING TO GET AWAY FROM THEM THAT I ALMOST FORGOT MY AMBITION. WOW, THAT WAS TOO CLOSE.

OH, YEAH, I FORGOT!

IT'S TOO RISKY TO BE SEEN WITH THESE GUYS. I MEAN, YOU *DO* WANT TO TAKE OVER THIS SCHOOL, DON'T YOU?

COULD THAT HAVE BEEN THEIR AIM? A *TRAP* TO DIMINISH MY REPUTATION?!

HOLD ON A SECOND!

NO, IT CAN'T BE. THEY ARE FAR TOO STUPID. THEY LOOK LIKE THEY'RE SERIOUS ABOUT ALL THIS.

THE ENEMY BOSS KNOWS?!

LISTEN, GUYS. MY FATHER HAS ALREADY FOUND US OUT.

ARE YOU OKAY?

I'LL HAVE TO THINK UP ANOTHER GOOD LIE!

AN AMERICAN ASSASSIN? THEY DON'T EVEN PUT THAT KINDA CRAP IN *MANGA* NOWADAYS.

OH, BROTHER, HERE WE GO AGAIN.

MY FATHER, THE DARK PRIME MINISTER, FEARS MY VERY EXISTENCE—SO MUCH IN FACT, THAT HE HAS ENLISTED THE AID OF AN EX-GREEN BERET TO ELIMINATE ME.

HOLY SMOKES! THEY BELIEVED *THAT*, TOO!

YEAH...

YOUR DAD MUST REALLY MEAN BUSINESS!

AN AMERICAN ASSASSIN?!

NICE ONE! DAMN, I'M GOOD!

SO I'M AFRAID I'LL BE LEAVING THE TEAM.

IF YOU HANG AROUND WITH ME, YOU'LL ONLY GET WRAPPED UP IN ALL THIS.

HUH? BUT I DON'T KNOW IF I CAN...

IT'S UP TO *YOU* NOW, KAMI-YAMA.

WELL, IT'S OBVIOUS.

BUT IF YOU QUIT, WHO'S GONNA BE THE CAPTAIN?

FREDDIE!

clasp

SWP

H... HAYASHIDA-KUN

YOU CAN DO IT.

HOW DID THIS EVER HAPPEN?

FINALLY, I CAN GO HOME. I'M *EXHAUSTED*...

OKAY! I WILL!

HANG IN THERE, DUDE!

WITHOUT ANY BACKING OR SUPPORT, I'M NOTHING MORE THAN AN ORDINARY STUDENT. THEREFORE, I HAD TO COME UP WITH A DECEPTION TO FOOL THOSE MORONS. BUT BEFORE I KNEW IT, THEY HAD MADE ME THEIR *CAPTAIN!*

IT'S ALL BECAUSE I MISTAKENLY TRANSFERRED HERE INSTEAD OF *REGGIE SMITH* HIGH, WHERE MY FATHER ACTUALLY *IS* THE DIRECTOR.

K-CHAK

I'LL TELL THEM EVERYTHING TOMORROW! THEN I'LL CHANGE SCHOOLS AGAIN, AND SAY FAREWELL TO THOSE FOOLS!

NO, I CAN'T TAKE IT ANY MORE!

FOR CRYING OUT LOUD! WHO *KNOWS* WHAT WILL HAPPEN IF I KEEP UP THIS RIDICULOUS CHARADE?!

"FIGHT-ING FOR JUSTICE AGAINST THE DARK PRIME MINIS-TER!..."

I'M... HOME.

WELCOME BACK!

WHY, UH, THANK YOU VERY MUCH... CAPTAIN.

FROM NOW ON, WE'LL BE STAYING AT YOUR HOUSE, IN ORDER TO PROTECT YOU. AS **CAPTAIN**, I WILL NOT ALLOW YOU TO DIE A MEANINGLESS DEATH.

NOW WHAT THE HELL AM I SUPPOSED TO DO?

YEP, THIS IS ALL YOU, TOO.

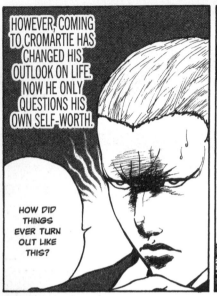

HOWEVER, COMING TO CROMARTIE HAS CHANGED HIS OUTLOOK ON LIFE. NOW HE ONLY QUESTIONS HIS OWN SELF-WORTH.

HOW DID THINGS EVER TURN OUT LIKE THIS?

AKIRA MAEDA (16) SINCE JUNIOR HIGH SCHOOL, HIS FIGHTING ABILITIES HAVE BEEN UNMATCHED. ALL HE HAS EVER BEEN CONCERNED ABOUT IS CLIMBING EVER HIGHER...

I KEPT RUNNING INTO THESE TOTAL BADASSES, ONE AFTER ANOTHER, AND BEFORE I KNEW IT, I WAS ONLY **AVERAGE**. ON TOP OF THAT, NOW EVERYONE THINKS I'M JUST A PART OF SOMEONE ELSE'S GANG.

WHEN I FIRST CAME TO THIS SCHOOL, I THOUGHT, "I'M GOIN' STRAIGHT TO THE TOP!" BUT NOW, THE THOUGHT ALONE EMBARRASSES ME. I COULDN'T **POSSIBLY** SAY SOMETHING LIKE THAT. (AND I'M GLAD I NEVER DID.)

HUH? HEY, YOU'RE HOKUTO'S HENCHMAN!

WELL, NOW. ARE YOU **REALLY** THAT STRONG?

HOW CAN I BE SO STRONG, AND NOT HAVE ANY KIND OF PRESENCE AT THIS SCHOOL?!

IF I LOSE CONTROL, I JUST DON'T LET UP. EVEN IF MY OPPONENT PASSES OUT, IT WON'T STOP ME FROM KICKIN' THE BASTARD WHILE HE'S DOWN! NOBODY EVER TRIES PICKING A FIGHT WITH **ME**!

I GUESS I'LL GO AHEAD AND TELL YOU--**EVERYONE** WHO KNEW WHO I WAS STEERED CLEAR OF ME!

YOU WERE THAT STRONG, BUT YOU DIDN'T HAVE A NICK-NAME?!

NO. I DIDN'T HAVE A NICK-NAME.

Sorry, that wasn't me.

DOES THIS MEAN YOU'RE... THE LEGENDARY **"RAGING WOLF"**?!

IS THAT RIGHT? I ALWAYS THOUGHT PUNKS WITH CRAZY NICKNAMES WERE SOMETHING YOU ONLY SAW IN MANGA.

YOU DON'T **NEED** ONE, BUT IF YOUR NAME IS, SAY, "THE BLACK PANTHER OF THE NORTH SEA," OR "THE ULTIMATE WEAPON OF KINSHI TOWN," YOU HAVE A LOT MORE **IMPACT.**

LET ME ASK YOU SOMETHING. WHAT'S SO IMPORTANT ABOUT HAVING A NICKNAME ANYWAY? ONCE I GOT MADE AN **ASS** OUT OF JUST 'CUZ I DIDN'T HAVE ONE. IT'S A PAINFUL MEMORY FOR ME... HEY, IF YOU'RE BAD, AND YOU'RE GOOD AT FIGHTING, ISN'T THAT ENOUGH?

WELL, WHAT IF **I** GAVE YOU ONE?

HMM... IN THAT CASE, **NOT** HAVING A NICKNAME ONLY MAKES THINGS HARDER.

WELL, YOU COULD ALWAYS SAY YOU WON THIS FIGHT, OR YOU WON THAT FIGHT, BUT IT'S A HECK OF A LOT EASIER TO SUM IT ALL UP WITH A SNAPPY NICKNAME, RIGHT?

THINGS LIKE THIS COME TO YOU THE SECOND YOU SEE THE GUY. FOR EXAMPLE, ON FIRST GLANCE YOU LOOK PRETTY **SHARP**, SO...

HOW THE HELL ARE **YOU** GONNA GIVE ME A NICKNAME? YOU DON'T EVEN FRICKIN' KNOW ME!

OKAY, WE CAN SHORTEN IT. MAYBE SOMETHING LIKE... **"THE DRAGON OF RAZORS."** HOW 'BOUT THAT?

THE DRAGON OF THE RAZORS... NAH, TOO LONG.

HOW ABOUT, **"THE DRAGON OF THE RAZORS"**?

COOL. I'M GLAD YOU LIKE IT.

HEY, THAT TOTALLY ROCKS!

THE DRAGON OF RAZORS...

SERIOUSLY, THOUGH. WHAT'S A GUY LIKE YOU DOIN' FOLLOWING A NIMROD LIKE HOKUTO?

HEY NOW. CUT THAT CRAP OUT.

I USED TO THINK EVERYONE HERE WAS A KNUCKLEHEAD, BUT THE SECOND I SAW YOU, I THOUGHT, "NAH, THIS GUY'S DIFFERENT."

I HATE TO SAY IT, BUT YOU LOOK MORE LIKE A **TOADY** THAN A FRIEND.

Didn't get a thing, though...

I FIGURED I'D BENEFIT FROM BEING BUDDIES WITH HIM, SINCE HE'S RICH AND INFLUENTIAL.

WE'VE ALWAYS BEEN FRIENDS.

IS THAT RIGHT? GUESS YOU'RE NOT TOO LUCKY YOURSELF.

AND BEFORE I KNEW IT, I GOT SUCKED IN AND WAS SPEAKING TO HIM ALL FORMAL... THE REST IS HISTORY.

WELL, AT FIRST WE WERE ON EQUAL TERMS. BUT THEN HE STARTED CALLIN' ME SHIT LIKE "YOU PEON," OR "YOU RAPSCALLION," LIKE WE WERE IN A SAMURAI DRAMA OR SOMETHING!

I SEE WHAT YOU'RE SAYING.

I JUST DON'T WANT YOU TO GET THE WRONG IDEA.

BUT I'VE NEVER CONSIDERED HITTING HIM UP FOR MONEY! MY FAMILY'S NOT RICH, BUT WE'RE NOT POOR, EITHER. GUESS YOU COULD SAY WE'RE UPPER-MIDDLE CLASS.

THERE'S ONLY ONE ANSWER.

IN ANY CASE, NOW I'VE BEEN LABELED AS A TOADY. I'M NOT GONNA HAVE ANY KIND OF **PRESENCE** OF MY OWN!

NOW I'M PUMPED! THINK OF SOMETHIN' **AWESOME!**

THIS TIME, LET ME GIVE YOU ONE.

THAT'S RIGHT! HEY, YOU'RE PRETTY SMART!

A NICK-NAME!

THE AMERICAN DREAM...

OKAY... I'VE GOT IT! FROM NOW ON, YOU ARE **"THE AMERICAN DREAM."**

JUST FOR A SECOND, I WAS KINDA LIKE, "HUH?" BUT I THINK THAT'S A NAME YOU COULD GET USED TO EASY!

I wanted to use it myself...

WELL I'M GLAD YOU LIKE IT.

DAMN, THAT ROCKS!

THE AMERICAN DREAM AND THE DRAGON OF... UH, SOMETHING-OR-OTHER, WE'RE GONNA TAKE OVER THE WORLD!

DUDE, SWEET! WE'RE PARTNERS IN CRIME!

THESE NICKNAMES SAY, "HEY, YOU'RE NOT GONNA CATEGORIZE US!"

GO FOR IT! 'CUZ THERE'S SOMETHING I GOTTA ASK YOU, TOO!

BY THE WAY! BEFORE WE TAKE OVER THE WORLD, I GOTTA ASK YA SOMETHING!

UH, WHAT'S YOUR REAL NAME?

GAH! WE DON'T HAVE **ANY** SORT OF PRESENCE AFTER ALL!!

HEY, YOU GUYS ARE SUPPORTING CAST.

CHAPTER SEVENTEEN: **CROMARTIE**

ENOUGH, ALREADY! FIRST IT'S FREDDIE, THEN THE GORILLA... SORRY, BUT I'VE SEEN SO MANY DIFFERENT TYPES AT THIS SCHOOL, NOTHING CAN FAZE ME ANYMORE!

KAMIYAMA! THERE'S THIS **TOTALLY WILD DUDE** IN ONE OF THE OTHER CLASSES!

COME ON, ALREADY!

WHAT, YOU THINK I GOT NOTHING BETTER TO DO. THIS AIN'T FOR YOUR ENTERTAINMENT, YA KNOW!

YOU'RE ALWAYS FINDING THESE "TOTALLY WILD DUDES." ARE YOU ACTUALLY BRINGING THEM IN FROM SOMEWHERE?

WHEN I SAW FREDDIE, THEN THE GORILLA, I THOUGHT, "WHAT'S NEXT, A NEANDERTHAL MAN?" IT'S LOST ITS NOVELTY!

THAT'S WHAT YOU ALWAYS SAY.

IT'S SO WILD. I NEVER SAW A GUY LIKE THIS.

RATTLE

YES, YES. LET'S JUST GET IT OVER WITH!

HEH. THAT'S WHAT **YOU** THINK.

NOTHING CAN SURPRISE ME NOW.

...

CHECK IT OUT.

MECHA-ZAWA?!

What's wrong?

HEY, BAD NEWS, MECHA-ZAWA!

I'M AT A LOSS FOR WORDS...

WELL? HOW 'BOUT **THAT?**

RIGHT! SO **NOW** WHAT DO WE DO?!

Sekine... He's Destrade's #2, right?

YESTERDAY, SUGAWARA GOT INTO IT WITH SOME GUYS FROM DESTRADE HIGH, BUT THEN **SEKINE** GOT INVOLVED!

HUH?!

Wait.

K-SHNK

HELL WITH IT! ONLY THING TO DO IS GET OUR GUYS TOGETHER AND GO **BUST SOME ASS!**

Besides... I'll bet Sugawara's the one who started it. Listen, I've got a buddy at Destrade. Maybe I can get him to smooth things over for us, and it'll all be water under the bridge.

You can't blame Sekine for steppin' in if somebody's giving his boys trouble. I don't think he's tryin' to start a war or anything.

YEAH. YOU'RE NO **WEAKLING,** BUT IT MIGHT BE HARD TO LIVE THIS ONE DOWN.

BUT... WHY'RE YOU ALWAYS TAKING THE HEAT LIKE THAT?

Don't worry. I might look like a wimp, but it ain't no shame for Cromartie.

WHAT? SO WE GONNA WIMP OUT?

*THEY **RELY** ON HIM.*

Ah, cut it out.

YOU'RE A HELL OF A GUY!

S... SORRY, MECHA-ZAWA. I JUST COULDN'T RESIST.

Ya frickin' moron! Didn't I tell ya to stay away from drugs?!

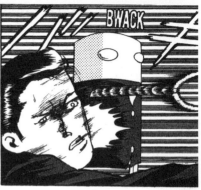

MECHA-ZAWA CARES ABOUT YOU MORE THAN ANYONE, DUDE.

I'M SORRY...

but, if you're gone, who the hell's gonna take care of your mom, huh?!

I couldn't care less about your sorry ass...

SQUIK SQUIK

Ah, can it!

NO ONE CAN BEAT MECHA-ZAWA!

MECHA-ZAWA'S THE BRAINS OF OUR CLASS.

HE'S GIVING SOUND ADVICE.

CREAK

What is it?

MECHA-ZAWA, WE GOTTA TALK.

HE'S OILING HIMSELF!!

AT LAST! SOMEONE'S GOING TO SAY IT!

THERE'S BEEN SOMETHING ON MY MIND EVER SINCE I LAID EYES ON YOU, BACK ON THE FIRST DAY OF CLASS.

I DUNNO... MAYBE YOU'VE EVEN NOTICED YOURSELF. BUT THEN AGAIN, MAYBE YOU HAVEN'T.

EVERYONE IN OUR CLASS IS PROBABLY THINKIN' THE SAME THING. I FIGURE EVEN PEOPLE ON THE **STREET** MIGHT NOTICE WHEN THEY SEE YOU.

FAMILY?

Hey, I think of us all as family. You can say whatever you like.

IT'S, UH, HARD TO SAY IT...

P-TNK

Well, what is it?

OKAY, MECHA-ZAWA, I'M GONNA SAY IT.

COME ON! SAY IT!!

FINE, THEN I'LL TELL IT TO YA STRAIGHT.

O.K.

NO, THAT'S NOT IT!!

And it's really been buggin' me...

YOUR MIDDLE BUTTON'S MISSING.

Ah! No kidding!

I never even noticed.

CHAPTER EIGHTEEN: **BLADE RUNNER'S HIGH**

DOO-DA

DA-DUM

IT JUST STOPPED. IS THIS THING BROKE AGAIN?!

WHAT'S THE MATTER?

HUH?

YEAH, RIGHT! THIS WHOLE SCHOOL'S A BUNCH OF **IDIOTS**!

WONDER IF ANYONE HERE COULD FIX IT...

AND I GOTTA **PAY** TO HAVE IT FIXED.

STUPID THING'S ALWAYS BREAKIN' ON ME.

HEY! I'LL BET **HE'S** GOOD WITH THAT STUFF!

GOOD WITH MACHINES, HUH?

HMM.

BUT ALMOST EVERY CLASS HAS A GUY WHO'S GOOD WITH MACHINES!

HEY, MECHAZAWA!

...

Huh?

CLASS 1-5, **SHINICHI MECHAZAWA (16)**

I'm just no good with machines.

Nah, no way.

THINK YOU CAN FIX THIS CD PLAYER?

HM?

VWEEE

HEY, YOU GOT A SECOND?

HE'S NO GOOD WITH MACHINES?!

Nah, I'm tellin' ya I can't!

Thought maybe you could help ME, too...

YA THINK YOU **COULD** JUST SHOW ME HOW TO **PROGRAM** IT?

I'VE TRIED EVERYTHING, BUT I CAN'T GET THIS VCR TO WORK! I'VE ALWAYS SUCKED WITH ELECTRONICS...

YEAH, RIGHT!!

Machines and I have just never gotten along.

I want to help you guys in any way I can--even if I gotta put my life on the line!

YOU'RE ALWAYS PRETTY HELPFUL, YA KNOW?

HMM. WELL, IT'S JUST...

Why are you bringing me your electronics?

YEAH, **RIGHT!!**

But when it comes to **machines**, I'm helpless myself.

It's like this--back in the day, people used to think women weren't any good with machines. But that was the same sort of preconceived notion.

And you're just making assumptions!

YOU JUST SEEM LIKE YOU'D BE GOOD WITH THAT STUFF.

See? You're prone to developing the wrong ideas with that sort of thinking.

squik
squik

THEY'RE AT LEAST 10 TIMES BETTER THAN US!

OH, I GET IT!

These days, women know how to use cell phones and email better than most men.

As for me, I'm not into the whole digital age thing. I just don't put much stock in that stuff.

HE'S OILING HIMSELF AGAIN!

The way things are goin', machines will end up taking over our lives!!

GOOD ADVICE AS USUAL, MAN.

Nothing can replace human interaction. Like talking face-to-face.

What is it?

VWEEE

HEY, MECHAZAWA. WE GOTTA TALK...

THAT WAS A *JOKE* JUST NOW, RIGHT?!

IT GETS TO ME EVERY TIME I SEE YA. LATELY, I'VE EVEN BEEN LOSIN' **SLEEP** OVER IT.

Not this again!

UH, WELL... EVER SINCE I MET YOU, THERE'S SOMETHING I JUST CAN'T GET OFF MY MIND.

I JUST DIDN'T KNOW HOW I'D BREAK IT TO YA.

Along with the chumps readin' this manga.

EVERYONE ELSE IS PROBABLY THINKING THE SAME THING, TOO...

IS HE *FINALLY* GOING TO SAY IT?

OKAY, THEN LISTEN UP, 'CUZ I'LL ONLY SAY THIS ONCE.

YES, SAY IT! QUICK!!

It's o.k.! Just say it!

I DON'T WANT TO HURT YOUR FEELINGS, THOUGH ...

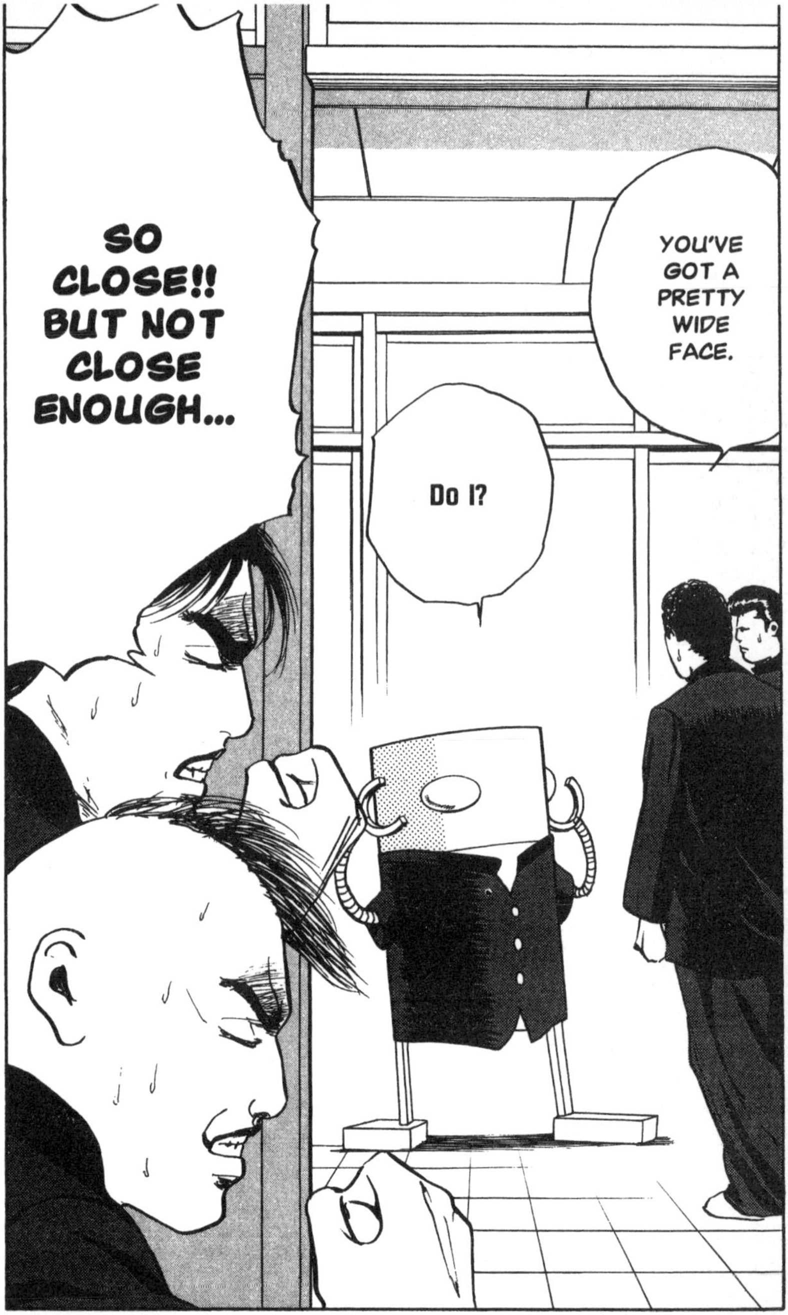
YOU'VE GOT A PRETTY WIDE FACE.
Do I?
SO CLOSE!! BUT NOT CLOSE ENOUGH...

OPERATION ATTRACT YOUNG READERS: MISSION FAILED

GORILLA

It may seem absurd to give this character a profile, but here he is, a gorilla. His appearance has cast a shadow of doubt over this manga. The issue is not whether he is a punk or delinquent or anything along those lines; whether he is actually even a *student* at Cromartie remains a mystery. This character's original name was Hiromi Go... but why? Somehow or other he gets along well with Freddie, and the two have even exchanged phone numbers. It has also been proven that he is at least smarter than Hayashida. His motto is "Banana" (Probably).

TAKESHI HOKUTO

Son of the wealthy and influential Hokuto family. For his ideals' sake, he aimed to take over Cromartie by using the political power his father holds as school director. However, his father is the director of *another* school, making Hokuto a mere "normal student whose father is the director at some other school." One would think he'd have realized Cromartie is a public school, and therefore has no director... He has ended up another totally silly character who hangs around with Kamiyama's group. However, this is not to say he has given up his original ambitions. His feudal lord style of talk has elicited guffaws from readers. One other thing (which the author had completely forgotten) is that Hokuto is more or less Kamiyama's rival. His motto is, "In all of heaven and earth, holy am I alone."

HOKUTO'S HENCHMAN →

He transferred with Hokuto in order to take over Cromartie. He is treated as nothing more than a lackey, even though he is actually quite strong. Not only does he have absolutely no presence, but nobody knows his name either. In fact, the author himself is ashamed to have referred to this character as "Uh, Hokuto's henchman," when speaking with the editors. Of course, Kamiyama and the others don't know his name, either. He has a fairly nondescript appearance, but this itself may be a defining characteristic, since everything around him is so much more evil. His motto is, "Life is harsh, and people are out to get you." He continues to refer to his classmate, Hokuto, as Hokuto-san. Cheers to his loyalty! Now, what to name him...

← SHINICHI MECHAZAWA

People seem to find this robot delinquent a bit unbelievable; however, both male and female readers are enamored of Mechazawa for his cerebral and down-to-earth remarks. But whatever way you look at it, Mechazawa is a robot—though he obnoxiously tries to play himself off as human. Since our font is quite a bit different, he was a big pain for the editors. Actually, since this manga has little popularity among elementary schoolers (LOL), I introduced him as the solution. In the end, my plan backfired, and I failed to capture the hearts of those youngsters. Naturally! His motto is, "I'm only human." Yeah right.

CHAPTER NINETEEN: **IN THE PURSUIT OF HIGHER LEARNING**

ACTUALLY, SINCE CLASSES BEGAN, I'VE GOTTEN MYSELF INTO ALL SORTS OF SITUATIONS...

YOU'LL BE OKAY. YOU'RE **SMART**, KAMIYAMA.

CRAP, I AIN'T READY AT ALL.

THE DAY BEFORE FINALS

I KNOW! WHAT WE NEED IS TO HAVE A CRAM SESSION AT MAEDA'S HOUSE!

I DON'T WANNA FLUNK! NOT **HERE**...

AND I JUST REALIZED I HAVEN'T EVEN STUDIED **ONCE** ALL SEMESTER.

JUST ONE QUESTION-- WHY **MY** PLACE?

OKAY! EVERYONE'S HERE, RIGHT?

MAEDA'S HOUSE

LET'S START WITH THE MULTIPLICATION TABLE!

THERE WON'T BE STUFF LIKE THAT ON **OUR** EXAMS!

WE'LL START WITH **MATH**. AT THE VERY LEAST, I FEEL WE SHOULD COVER FACTORIZATION, AND DIFFERENTIAL AND INTEGRAL EQUATIONS.

BUT IT'S **GRADE SCHOOL** LEVEL!

NOT REALLY.

YOU'RE TALKING THE ABSOLUTE **BASICS**. YOU MUST KNOW THAT MUCH AT LEAST!

SINCE ANTIQUITY, MY FAMILY HAS PASSED DOWN KNOWLEDGE OF A MEMORIZATION TECHNIQUE KNOWN AS **THE MYSTICAL MNEMONIC**. USE IT, AND YOU SHALL NEVER FORGET WHAT YOU COMMIT TO MEMORY!

HUH?

HEH. LET **ME** HANDLE THIS.

STOP FOOLING AROUND, HOKUTO-KUN.

HOWEVER! I REGRET TO SAY I **FORGOT** THE TECHNIQUE.

HOW IN THE WORLD DOES IT WORK?

I NEVER HEARD OF SOMETHING SO **RAD!**

MAEDA-KUN IS DRIVING A BUS. HOKUTO-KUN AND HIS HENCHMAN GET ON. THEN TAKENOUCHI-KUN BOARDS, BUT FALLS ILL AND HAS TO GET OFF IMMEDIATELY. AFTER THAT, HOKUTO-KUN'S HENCHMAN GETS OFF, TOO. HOW MANY PEOPLE ARE RIDING THE BUS NOW?

RIGHT!

OKAY, I'LL ASK AN EASY QUESTION. SEE IF YOU CAN ANSWER IT.

HAYASHIDA-KUN... IT'S NOT A **RIDDLE**. I'M ASKING HOW MANY PEOPLE ARE ON THE BUS!!

THE BUS DRIVER'S NAME IS **MAEDA**!

I... I GOT IT!

TH... THAT'S RIGHT!

HM?

STOP IT, HAYASHIDA-KUN! NOW **YOU'RE** ACTING LIKE AN ANIMAL!

YOU DIRTY BASTARD! YOU WERE ONLY **ACTING** LIKE YOU AIN'T BEEN STUDYIN'!

THE **EQUATION** IS 3 X 2 = 6. GOT IT?

THIS ISN'T **DIFFICULT!** OKAY, LET'S SAY MANDARIN ORANGES COME IN PACKS OF THREE, AND YOU HAVE TWO PACKS. HOW MANY ORANGES DO YOU HAVE IN ALL?

WHEN YOU TALK ABOUT ALL THOSE NUMBERS AND SYMBOLS AND STUFF, IT GETS TO ME. I KINDA **PANIC**, YA KNOW?

SURE, I GET IT, BUT...

OTHER THAN HAYASHIDA-KUN, THE REST OF YOU UNDERSTAND, RIGHT?

HM?

HAYASHIDA-KUN.

I SEE. I SHOULD USE SOMETHING OTHER THAN PLAIN NUMERALS. HMM, MAYBE IF I...

HE USED SOMETHING HAYASHIDA IS ACTUALLY **INTERESTED** IN!

SO **THAT'S** IT!

SAY YOU CHECKED OUT ELEVEN ADULT VIDEOS. THREE OF THOSE WERE NEW RELEASES, SO YOU HAD TO RETURN THEM THE NEXT DAY. HOW MANY VIDEOS DO YOU HAVE LEFT?

HOW ABOUT THIS, THEN? YOU'RE IN A RAID ON DESTRADE HIGH SCHOOL. YOU FACED OFF AGAINST FIVE OPPONENTS, AND TOOK OUT TWO WITH A WEAPON. HOW MANY DO YOU HAVE LEFT?

YOU SHOULD BE ABLE TO ANSWER THAT ONE WITHOUT EVEN **THINKING!**

LOOK, I'M TELLIN' YA I JUST DON'T GET THIS KIND OF STUFF.

IT LOOKS LIKE TRYING TO **EXPLAIN** IT WON'T DO ANY GOOD. MAYBE IT'S JUST SOMETHING YOU GOTTA LEARN BY **DOING.**

YOU CAN'T EVEN SUBTRACT TWO FROM FIVE?

YOU DON'T THINK ABOUT THAT STUFF IN THE MIDDLE OF A **FIGHT!**

I don't like where this is headed...

THEN I GUESS IT'S TIME WE MADE A RAID ON DESTRADE.

...

OKAY! NOW I'M READY TO ROCK!

THIS IS FOR THE TEST!

YEAH

I'M FUNDAMEN-TALLY AGAINST FIGHTING. BUT IF IT WILL HELP HAYASHIDA-KUN UNDERSTAND MATH, THEN THERE'S NO CHOICE.

WELL, KAMI-YAMA?

DESTRADE HIGH SCHOOL

RIGHT ON!!

LET'S DO IT!!

THE DAY OF THE EXAM

I knew it...

ALL WERE SUSPENDED FROM SCHOOL FOR FIGHTING.

YEAH, THAT'S ABOUT RIGHT.

YEAH, DON'T SCREW WITH BASS!

WHACK

CRACK Ungh

DON'T PUSH IT, SHRIMP!

Urgh

...

OH, MAN! MECHAZAWA'S GETTING HIS ASS KICKED!

SMACK

HUH? WHY NOT?!

NO, WAIT! WE CAN'T GET INVOLVED!

KAMIYAMA! WE GOTTA HELP HIM!

OH, YEAH! THEN WE SHOULD STAY HERE AND WATCH LIKE WE ALWAYS DO, RIGHT?

FOR SOME REASON, I GET THE FEELING THESE GUYS MIGHT **SAY IT!**

HEY, IF YA WANNA APOLOGIZE, NOW'S THE TIME!

THIS GUY CAN TAKE A BEATIN'.

BA-WHACK

HEY, KAMIYAMA. I JUST HAD A FREAKY THOUGHT.

WHAT IS IT?

WHAT? YOU SONNUVA...

This ain't enough to do me in.

WELL, EVERYONE BESIDES US SEEMS TO THINK HE'S A NORMAL HIGH SCHOOL **PUNK**.

WHAT DO YOU MEAN?

WHAT IF **WE'RE** THE ONLY ONES WHO HAVE ANY DOUBTS ABOUT MECHAZAWA?

YEAH! WE GOT A SCORE TO SETTLE WITH YOU!

CLANG

WHACK

I'LL FRICKIN' **KILL** YA!

BUT HE JUST DOESN'T **LOOK** LIKE A HIGH SCHOOLER-- OR A **HUMAN** FOR THAT MATTER!

I mean, he doesn't even have a nose or mouth!

CRACK

CLANG

RIGHT! MECHAZAWA'S JUST A NORMAL 16-YEAR-OLD. THERE'S NO OTHER WAY TO EXPLAIN IT!

SO... YOU THINK **WE** MIGHT HAVE THE WRONG IDEA?

YEAH! THERE'S ALWAYS A FEW DOWN ON CENTER STREET!

WELL... I SUPPOSE THERE ARE OTHERS LIKE HIM OUT THERE...

GRR! YOU GOT A BIG MOUTH!

Heh. what, is that all?

SHUT THE HELL UP! HE ASKED FOR IT!

WHOA, MAN! TAKE IT EASY!

FWICK

HUH?

CLANK

WHAT?! THAT MUST MEAN...

WHAT THE HELL? MY KNIFE BENT...

H-HE **AIN'T** *HUMAN* AFTER ALL!

YES! THIS IS OUR MAN! SAY IT!!

WE THOUGHT MECHAZAWA WAS A NORMAL GUY, BUT **MAYBE...**

YOU'RE JOKING! RIGHT?!

WHOA, SO, LIKE, HIS BODY'S **CRAZY** HARD, HUH?

YA GOT A PRETTY FRICKIN' HARD BODY, DONTCHA?!

I guess since you're a bunch of pansy-ass bitches, all ya can do is fight in a pack.

WHAT WAS THAT?

None of you have the guts to take me on alone, huh?

YOKOYAMA-KUN!

IT'S LIKE HE SAYS.

HE'S TALKING AS COOL AS USUAL!

I MEAN, LOOK AT YA! FIVE OR SIX OF YOU ROUGHIN' UP **ONE GUY**... PATHETIC!

BUT...

IT'S TRUE THERE AIN'T NO RULES IN A FIGHT, BUT YA THINK YOU COULD AT LEAST SHOW SOME **HONOR?!**

WH... **WHAT?!**

: : :

YOU OVERDID IT! LOOK AT 'IM!

DON'T YA HAVE ANY **PRIDE?**

YES! YOU'RE ALMOST THERE!

YOU'RE A R- R- R...

Y... YOU'RE A...

ALL RIGHT! THIS GUY'S GONNA SAY IT!

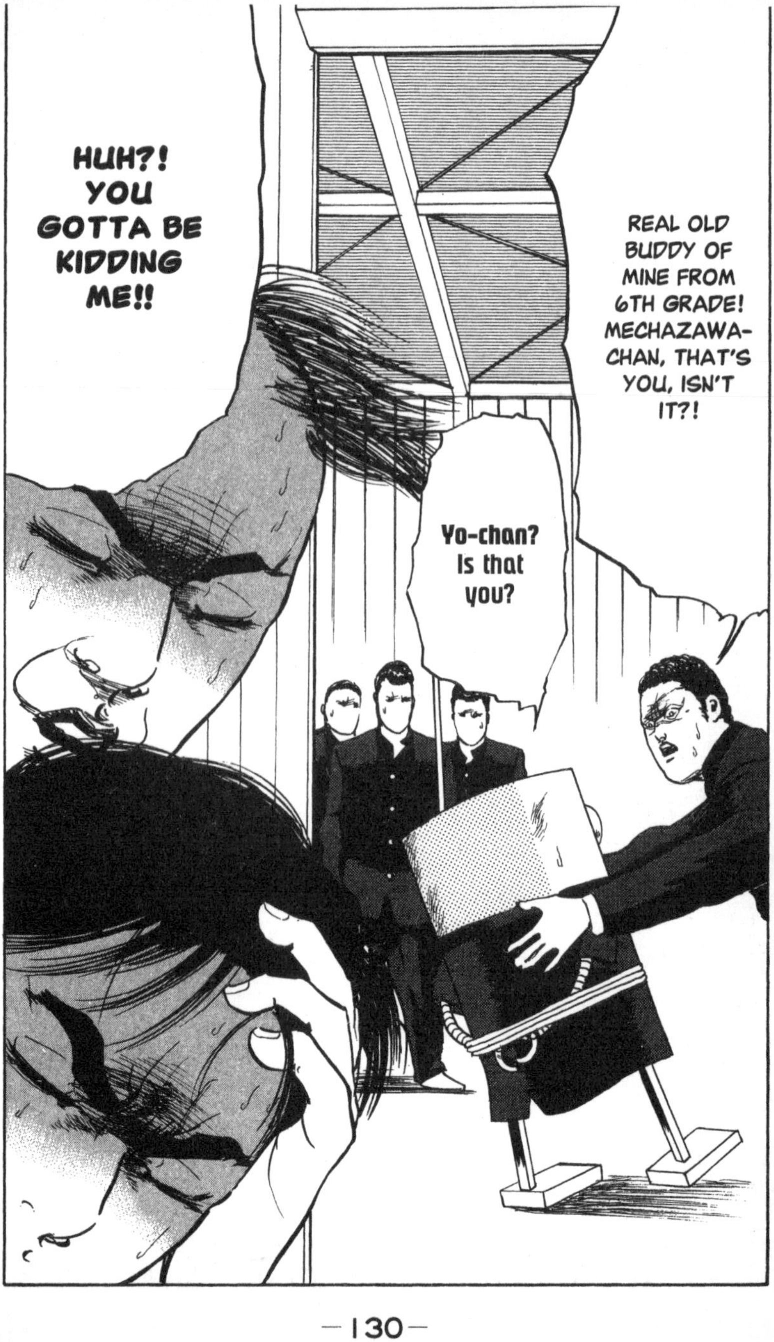
REAL OLD BUDDY OF MINE FROM 6TH GRADE! MECHAZAWA-CHAN, THAT'S YOU, ISN'T IT?!
Yo-chan? Is that you?
HUH?! YOU GOTTA BE KIDDING ME!!

WHAT KIND OF 6TH GRADER IS THAT?

CHAPTER TWENTY-ONE: **THE BIG CLEANUP**

A BIRTHDAY PARTY WAS BEING HELD AT MAEDA'S HOUSE.

♪ HAPPY BIRTHDAY TO YA.

YOU...

♪ HAPPY BIRTH-DAY TO YOU.

BIRTHDAY!

♪ A HAPPY...

WHY'S IT ALWAYS GOTTA BE AT MY PLACE?!

FREDDIE!!

♪

HUH?!

WELL, WE **DON'T** KNOW, SO WE DECIDED ON ONE FOR HIM TODAY.

HOW DO YOU EVEN KNOW IT'S HIS BIRTHDAY?!

MAN, THAT'S COLD.

...AND THAT'S ABOUT AS FAR AS I WROTE. THAT'S ALL FOR THIS PART. IT'S TOO MUCH OF A PAIN TO THINK OF HOW IT'LL END, SO NOW I'LL CONTINUE WITH ANOTHER LEFTOVER SCENARIO I HAD.

MY NAME IS YUTAKA TAKENOUCHI. I'M INSANELY STRONG, AND I'M THE UNDERGROUND KINGPIN OF THE 1ST YEAR STUDENTS AT CROMARTIE. MY SINGLE WEAKNESS IS THAT I GET MOTION SICK REAL EASY, SO I HAVE A FEAR OF VEHICLES.

YUTAKA TAKENOUCHI, ATTEMPTING TO RIDE THE BUS TO SCHOOL

VRMMM

DESPITE MY APPEARANCE, I AM INTELLIGENT, AS WELL AS STRONG. IN JUNIOR HIGH, I COULD EASILY SCORE IN THE 60S WITHOUT EVEN STUDYING.

SO YOU MAY WONDER WHY I CAME TO A LOSER SCHOOL LIKE CROMARTIE.

WELL, THE REASON IS...

I COULD RIDE A BIKE, BUT THAT WOULDN'T BE **COOL**. AND IN THE WORST CASE, I'D GET SICK ON THE BIKE, TOO.

BUT WALKING THERE STILL TAKES 15 MINUTES. IT GETS TIRING DAY AFTER DAY.

IT'S THE CLOSEST SCHOOL TO MY HOUSE.

A key factor, considering my motion sickness.

PLUS, I WON'T RUN INTO **THAT ASSHOLE** HERE.

JUST SEEING THE BUS FREAKED ME OUT AT FIRST, BUT I FIGURE I CAN HANDLE IT FOR AT LEAST A COUPLE STOPS. SOMEHOW OR OTHER I ALWAYS END UP RIDING VEHICLES ANYWAY...

VRMMM

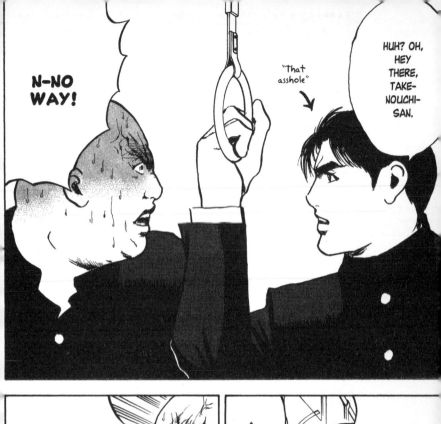

N-NO WAY!

"That asshole"

HUH? OH, HEY THERE, TAKE-NOUCHI-SAN.

IS YOUR HOUSE FAR FROM SCHOOL?! C'MON ASSHOLE, SPIT IT OUT!!

A REASON? BUT...

WHY THE HELL'RE **YOU** RIDING THE BUS?! GIVE ME A REASON! TELL ME **NOW!**

WELL, ACTUALLY, I...

THAT'S CLOSER THAN ME! SO WHY'RE YA TAKING THE BUS?!

WALKING, IT TAKES ME 10 MINUTES. ABOUT THREE IF I RIDE MY BIKE.

I JUST LOVE RIDING ON MOTOR VEHICLES.

♪

HAPPY BIRTHDAY TO YOU...

♪

HAPPY BIRTHDAY...

THAT'S ALL FOR THIS SCENE, TOO. IT SEEMED KIND OF HALF-ASSED, SO I'LL GO WITH A DIFFERENT SCENARIO NOW.

YEAA, HAPPY BIRTHDAY!

HAPPY BIRTHDAY, TAKENOUCHI-KUN!!

♪

I WAS VERY HAPPY DESPITE MYSELF, AND CASUALLY ACCEPTED.

THEY OFFERED TO HAVE A BIRTHDAY PARTY FOR ME.

IT MAY SEEM I'M REPEATING MYSELF, BUT I AM THE STRONGEST IN MY CLASS, AND THE UNDERGROUND KINGPIN OF CROMARTIE'S IST YEARS. YES, MY STRENGTH IS FIGHTING, BUT MY WEAKNESS IS RIDING IN VEHICLES.

MY NAME IS YUTAKA TAKENOUCHI.

HOWEVER.

THERE'S JUST ONE PROBLEM.

THEY DECIDED TO THROW THE PARTY...

ON A HOUSE-BOAT.

Houseboat

HE'S NOT THE CAPTAIN, TAKE-NOUCHI! DON'T HIT HIM!

WHOA, NOW HE'S FREAK-ING OUT!

STOP IT, FREDDIE!

URP.

OH, NO! TAKE-NOUCHI PASSED OUT!

I'M FINISHED CLEANING OUT MY SUPPLY OF LEFTOVER SCENARIOS.

THIS IS WHY I'VE CALLED YOU ALL HERE TODAY.

SLRP
ズ

HEH. SOMETIMES YOU **DO** MAKE SENSE, MOHAWK. I'LL BE DELIGHTED TO TAKE ANY OF YOU ON.

IT IS STILL NOT CLEAR WHO IS THE **STRONGEST** AMONG US.

WHAT?

HOLD ON.

I AM MORALLY OPPOSED TO SUCH VIOLENCE. WE SHOULD USE A MORE **PEACEFUL** METHOD!

BUT THERE'S SOMETHING I WANT TO TELL ALL OF YOU RIGHT NOW.

I UNDERSTAND WHY YOU WANT TO SEE WHO'S STRONGEST. BELIEVE ME, I CAN IDENTIFY...

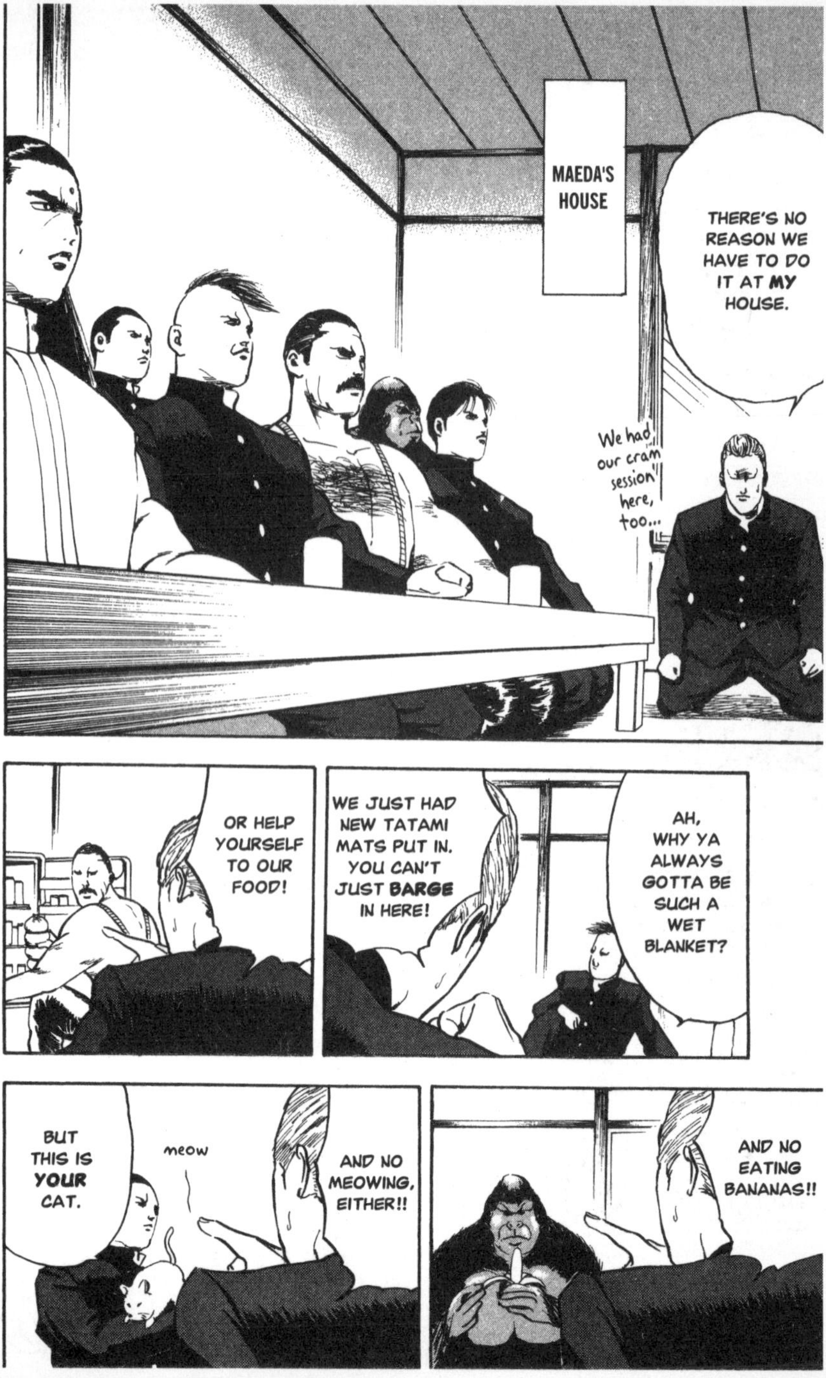
MAEDA'S HOUSE
THERE'S NO REASON WE HAVE TO DO IT AT MY HOUSE.
We had our cram session here, too...
AH, WHY YA ALWAYS GOTTA BE SUCH A WET BLANKET?
WE JUST HAD NEW TATAMI MATS PUT IN. YOU CAN'T JUST BARGE IN HERE!
OR HELP YOURSELF TO OUR FOOD!
AND NO EATING BANANAS!!
AND NO MEOWING, EITHER!!
meow
BUT THIS IS YOUR CAT.

YOU SHALL REGRET HASTENING YOUR OWN DEMISE.

SOUNDS LIKE FUN.

I GUESS WE'LL HAVE TO DO A ONE-ON-ONE ELIMINATION.

TO HELL WITH THAT! AND WHO LET **YOU** DECIDE, ANYHOW?

OKAY, THEN. THE FIRST MATCH WILL BE MAEDA VS. THE GORILLA.

LOOK, FORGET ABOUT FIGHTIN' IN HERE. IF YOU **HAVE** TO, GO OUTSIDE. I'M SERIOUS!

DAMN STRAIGHT! THIS IS **MY** HOUSE!!

YOU'RE SURE WALKIN' TALL TODAY.

I WILL KILL YOU.

WHAT?! BUT, I WANNA TEAR SHIT UP!

LET'S DECIDE THE STRONGEST THROUGH **NEGOTIA-TIONS.**

IF YOU KEEP THIS UP, I'M CALLIN' THE COPS!

BUT IT'S COLD OUT.

SOUNDS BORING, BUT IF THAT'S HOW IT IS...

FINE **BY** ME.

I'M SURE WE CAN REACH SOME CONCLUSION IF WE LOOK AT EVERYONE'S ACTUAL **COMBAT PERFORMANCE**, AS WELL AS THE DETAILS OF THE FIGHT AND ANY OTHER MARTIAL EXPLOITS.

LET US CLEARLY DETERMINE WHO IS THE STRONGEST IN THE **HOKUTO CORPS**.

VERY WELL!

WHAT? YOU MEAN YOU **AREN'T** IN THE HOKUTO CORPS?

WHERE THE HECK DID **THAT** COME FROM?

"HOKUTO CORPS"?

HUH?

UM... THAT WASN'T WHAT I HAD IN MIND.

PHYSICAL STRENGTH ASIDE, SOMETIMES YOU HAVE YOUR WAY JUST 'CUZ YOU **SAID SO!**

IN A WAY, HOKUTO-SAN IS THE MOST FIT TO LEAD US.

UH... THERE'S PROBABLY NOTHING WE **CAN** DO ABOUT THEM. BESIDES, I DON'T THINK THE GORILLA'S EVEN A **STUDENT.**

BUT WHAT DO WE DO ABOUT THESE TWO?

They don't talk.

HEY, WHEN DID YOU BECOME THE MODERATOR?

FIRST, LET'S HEAR EVERYONE'S OPINION.

THEN WHY DON'T YOU ALL GO HOME?!

YEAH. I'M SICK OF THIS.

WE'RE NEVER GONNA FIGURE IT OUT THIS WAY.

YEAH, TRUE ENOUGH!

I MEAN, IF YOU LOOK AT US AS A **WHOLE**, WE HAVE NOTHING TO FEAR, RIGHT?

LOOK, I DON'T REALLY KNOW WHO'S THE STRONGEST, BUT DOES IT REALLY **MATTER?**

RIGHT! THERE AIN'T A DAMN THING IN THE WORLD THAT CAN SCARE US!

THAT'S RIGHT! WITH A GROUP LIKE THIS, WE CAN TAKE ON **ANYONE** AND **ANYTHING!**

We even have a gorilla.

ACTUALLY, THIS **IS** A TOUGH GROUP.

NOW THAT IS FRICKIN' SCARY.

THAT'S MY MOM...

AND A FRIGHTENING RESEMBLANCE.

CHAPTER TWENTY-THREE: **MAEDA'S BIG DAY**

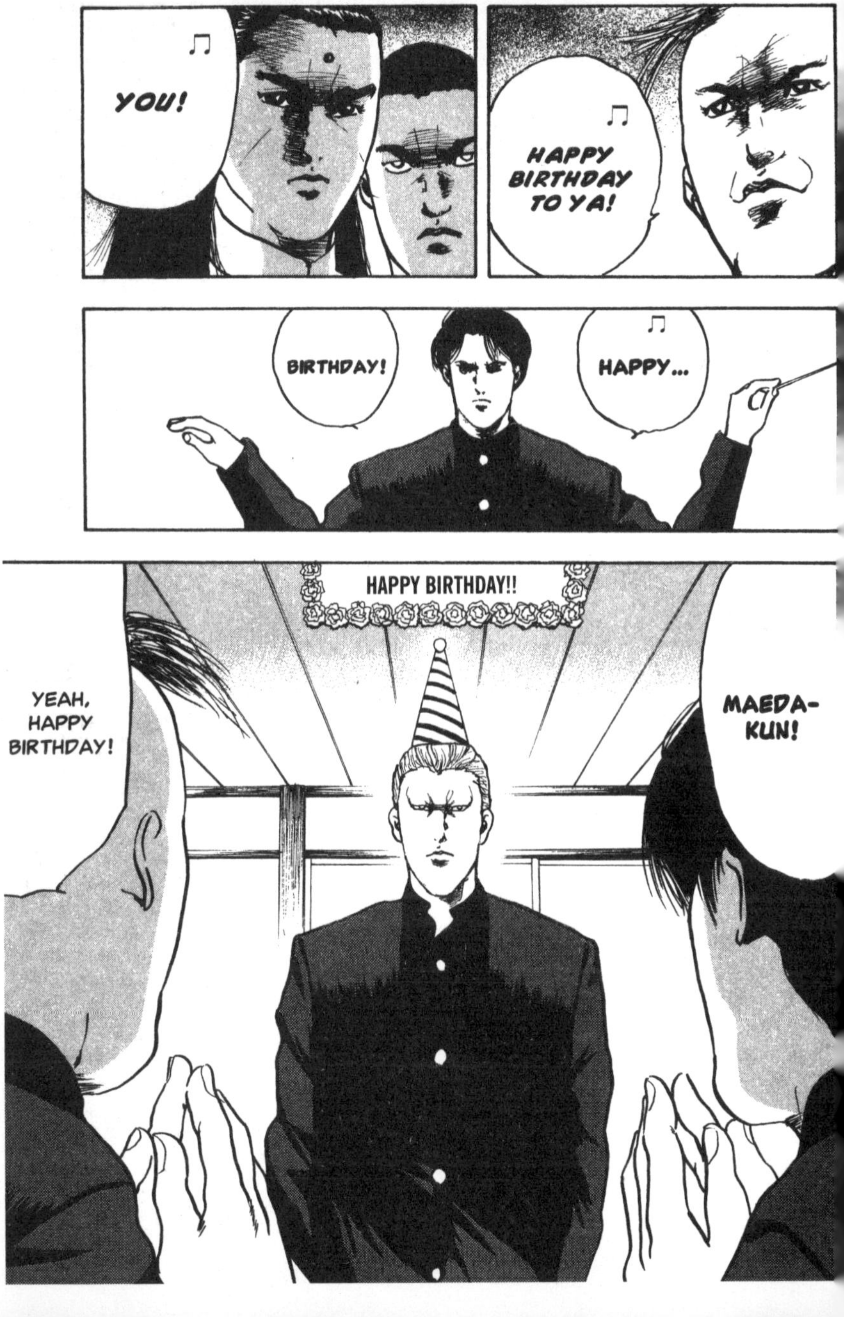
♫ HAPPY BIRTHDAY TO YA!
♫ YOU!
♫ HAPPY...
BIRTHDAY!
HAPPY BIRTHDAY!!
MAEDA-KUN!
YEAH, HAPPY BIRTHDAY!

IT'S OKAY TO LET LOOSE, BUT REMEMBER WE'RE AT **MAEDA'S** HOUSE! CALM DOWN, OR YOU'LL ONLY MAKE HIM...

HOLD ON, HAYASHIDA-KUN!

POP

ALL RIGHT! TIME TO **PARTY!!**

I MEAN, YOU'RE ALL HERE FOR **ME**, RIGHT?

HUH?

DON'T WORRY ABOUT IT, KAMIYAMA.

THIS MAKES ME REALLY HAPPY.

HEY, THAT'S MY LINE.

YEAH. I'M GLAD WE'RE FRIENDS.

YOU'RE OKAY WITH ME, MAN.

BUT TODAY THEY'RE ALL HERE TO CELEBRATE MY BIRTHDAY. THERE'S NO REASON FOR ME TO BE ANGRY. EVEN IF THEY DO GET A LITTLE NOISY, IT'S O.K.

THESE GUYS ARE ALWAYS OVER HERE ARGUING ABOUT WHO'S THE STRONGEST, OR HAVING "CRAM SESSIONS." THEY ACT LIKE THEY OWN THE PLACE. IT CAN BE A REAL PAIN IN THE ASS...

THERE'S JUST ONE THING I'D LIKE TO TELL THEM RIGHT NOW.

MY BIRTHDAY WAS **LAST** MONTH...

BUT IF I SAY THAT NOW, IT'LL ONLY SPOIL THE MOOD. IT WAS A SIMPLE MISTAKE. IT'S NOT LIKE THEY **MEANT** IT OR ANYTHING...

HAPPY BIRTH-DAY!

HUH?

THE NOTION **DOES** STRIKE MY FANCY...

WHY DON'T WE FINISH UP THE PARTY AND HEAD OVER THERE?

HEY, NOT TO CHANGE THE SUBJECT, BUT I HEARD SOME SINGER'S DOING AN AUTOGRAPH SIGNING TODAY. IT'S AT THAT BOOKSTORE OVER BY THE STATION.

WHAT ARE YOU GUYS TALKING ABOUT?! I THOUGHT YOU WERE HERE TO CELEBRATE MY BIRTHDAY!

DUDE, THAT'S MAEDA'S **MOM.**

THAT'S COOL, RIGHT, MAEDA?

HUH?

HAYA-SHIDA-KUN.

AARGH, I DON'T KNOW HOW TO SAY IT!

THAT'S WHAT I **WANT** TO ASK THEM... BUT IT'S NOT MY BIRTHDAY ANYWAY.

IN ALL MY LIFE, I'VE HIT A PERSON ONLY TWICE.

WHAT THE HELL WAS THAT?!

SMACK

THERE ARE SOME THINGS YOU SHOULD NEVER SAY, EVEN IF YOU ARE CLOSE TO SOMEBODY. IF YOU REALLY CARED ABOUT MAEDA-KUN, YOU SHOULDN'T HAVE SAID SUCH A THING! IT'S HIS **BIRTHDAY!** ARE YOU LISTENING TO ME?!

THOSE ARE THE ONLY TIMES I'VE BEEN TRULY ANGRY.

NO, HE'S RIGHT. I GOT TOO WORKED UP, AND SAID SOMETHIN' STUPID. EVEN A LITTLE THING LIKE THAT CAN HURT SOMETIMES.

IT'S NO BIG DEAL, KAMIYAMA, REALLY!

WELL, THEN. WE HAVE A LITTLE **PRESENT** FOR YOU.

GOOD. THAT TAKES CARE OF THAT.

STOP IT, MAN! THIS AIN'T LIKE YOU!

THINK YA CAN FORGIVE ME, MAEDA?

TH-THANKS, YOU GUYS. OKAY, I'LL BLOW 'EM ALL OUT WITH ONE BREATH!

sniff

clap
clap

TODAY'S **YOUR** DAY, SO WE HAD A CAKE MADE SPECIALLY FOR YOU! NOW, BLOW OUT THE CANDLES!

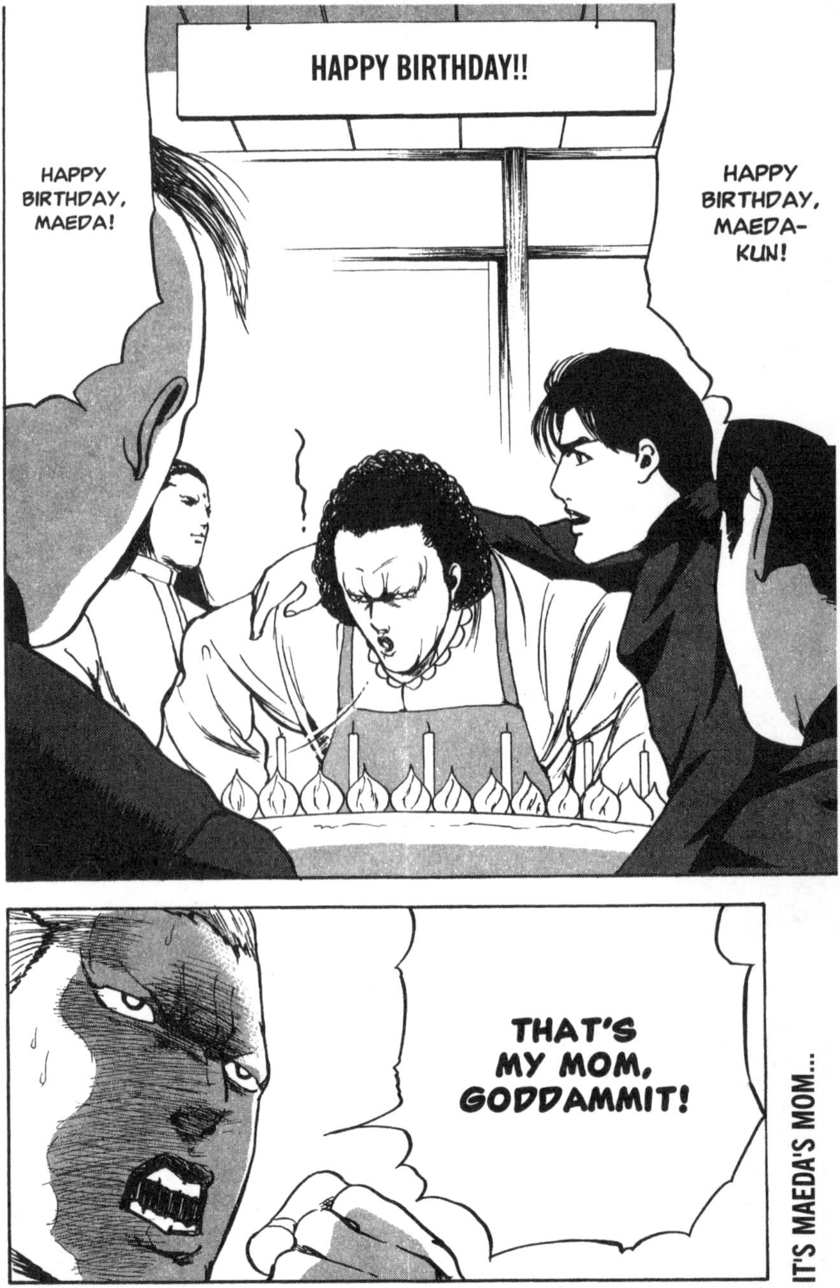
HAPPY BIRTHDAY!!
HAPPY BIRTHDAY, MAEDA-KUN!
HAPPY BIRTHDAY, MAEDA!
THAT'S MY MOM, GODDAMMIT!

IT'S MAEDA'S MOM...

VOLUME 1 • THE END

BONUS MANGA
VALIANTLY FORGE ONWARD! PRO WRESTLER BIOGRAPHY

WHEN YOU STEP INTO THAT RING, IT'S ALL ABOUT BEING AS **BAD** AS YOU CAN BE!

AH, YOU'RE JUST A ROOKIE.

I'VE ALWAYS BEEN TIMID, SO I'M WORRIED ABOUT DOING THIS "SMACK TALK."

THERE WERE A COUPLE TIMES IN THE PAST WHEN I FORGOT TO DO THAT. MAKES THINGS REAL AWKWARD...

AND DON'T FORGET TO SWITCH THE MIC ON!

YES, SIR!

AH, NOTHIN'. JUST TRYING TO GET THE CAP OFF THIS BOTTLE.

BY THE WAY, SEMPAI, WHAT ARE YOU DOING?

PRO WRESTLING IS SCARY, ISN'T IT?

SOME GUYS'LL TURN IT OFF ON YOU AS A TRICK.

ANYHOW, THE POINT IS, BEING A PRO WRESTLER'S ALL ABOUT SHOWING 'EM WHAT KIND OF **POWER** YOU GOT!!

GET OUTTA HERE! YOU THINK IF **I** CAN'T OPEN IT, **YOU** CAN?!

SHALL I OPEN IT FOR YOU?

RRNGH...

OKAY.

HERE, GO AHEAD AND TRY.

NRGH...

NO WAY!

GOT IT.

OF COURSE, SINCE I DIDN'T HAVE ANY LUCK, I DOUBT YOU'LL...

I'M SORRY?

HEY, MAKE NO MISTAKE, PAL.

YOU'RE ABSOLUTELY RIGHT.

NOT THAT YOU HAVE **POWER** OR ANYTHING.

YOU ONLY GOT IT BECAUSE I ALREADY LOOSENED IT UP WITH MY **POWER**.

IT ONLY NEEDED ANOTHER LITTLE TWIST, AND THAT'S JUST WHAT YOU GAVE IT. A LITTLE TWIST.

OKAY... I'M NOT SURE I UNDERSTAND, THOUGH.

THERE! **NOW** TRY TO OPEN IT!

WHY ARE YOU PUTTING IT BACK ON?

twist twist twist

THAT'S THE BIGGEST DANGER FOR PRO WRESTLERS. FIRST YOU TAKE OFF A CAP THAT'S ON TOO TIGHT, THEN YOU THINK YOU'RE WHERE IT'S AT, BUT WHAT YOU LOSE SIGHT OF IS...

I DON'T WANT YOU OVERESTIMATING YOUR OWN STRENGTH JUST BECAUSE YOU OPENED A BOTTLE.

NO WAY!

GOT IT.

IT'S EASY TO TAKE A CAP OFF, BUT THE **HARD** PART IS PUTTING IT **ON.**

SEE WHAT?

AH, NOW I SEE!

GRRGH...

SHOULDN'T YOU DRINK IT FIRST, THOUGH?

THIS TIME, **YOU** PUT IT BACK ON.

OKAY. NOW I'LL **OPEN** IT.

YOU TIGHTENED IT TOO MUCH! NOW IT'LL NEVER COME OFF.

≡HUFF≡
≡HUFF≡

: : :
: : :

BWEH!!

GOT IT.

'CUZ SOMETHING LIKE THAT STUPID **BOTTLE CAP** DOESN'T HAVE ANYTHING TO DO WITH BEING **STRONG!**

I WASN'T THINKING THAT AT ALL.

DO YOU ACTUALLY THINK YOU'RE STRONGER THAN **ME?**

NO, NOT AT ALL...

YOU'RE NOT AFTER MY BELT, ARE YOU?

NO... NEVER.

YOU EVER SEE WRESTLERS GET OUT THERE IN THE RING AND START OPENING **BOTTLES?** WELL, HAVE YA?!

I'M SURE I COULD ONLY OPEN IT BECAUSE OF YOUR HELP, SEMPAI.

I... I'M SORRY.

AH, MAN, YA SPOILED MY MOOD. I DON'T EVEN FEEL LIKE FIGHTIN' NOW.

LISTEN UP. I'LL SHOW YOU WHAT **WRESTLING POWER** IS ALL ABOUT!

OH. SORRY.

I'M TELLIN' YA, THE DAMN BOTTLE DOESN'T HAVE ANYTHING TO DO WITH IT!

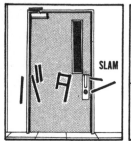

SLAM

I'LL BE SURE TO REMEMBER!

IT'S NOT ABOUT BOTTLE CAPS! GET THAT INTO YOUR HEAD!

バタン
p-cht

k-chk
カチャ

WOW, THAT WAS REALLY QUICK! HOW DID THE MATCH GO?

HUH?

HUH?! YOU MEAN YOU'RE A **MASKED WRESTLER**?!

I FORGOT TO PUT ON MY **MASK**...

MEN ARE NOT BOTTLE CAPS.

THE END

MANGA I DREW IN 5 MINUTES

Then one day I picked up a beret I found on the side of the road.

Later on, I learned a certain famous manga author wore that kind of hat.

I AM MANGA AUTHOR EIJI NONAKA. WHEN IT COMES TO MANNERS AND MODESTY, NO ONE CAN HOLD A CANDLE TO ME.

Nope. I delivered it to the police.

I see. And that was your impetus to become a manga artist?

I have only one weakness.

Interviewer

I don't really like manga that much.

Yes. I suppose you're right.

Hey. No one's gonna become a manga artist because of something like that.

Today, I will tell you about that.

Why did I ever become a manga artist?

It was a Hi-Fi SVHS recorder, which was pretty rare back then.

Then 10 years later, I found a VCR.

I hated books. I never even read any manga.

Back in childhood, I was the biggest trouble-maker in town.

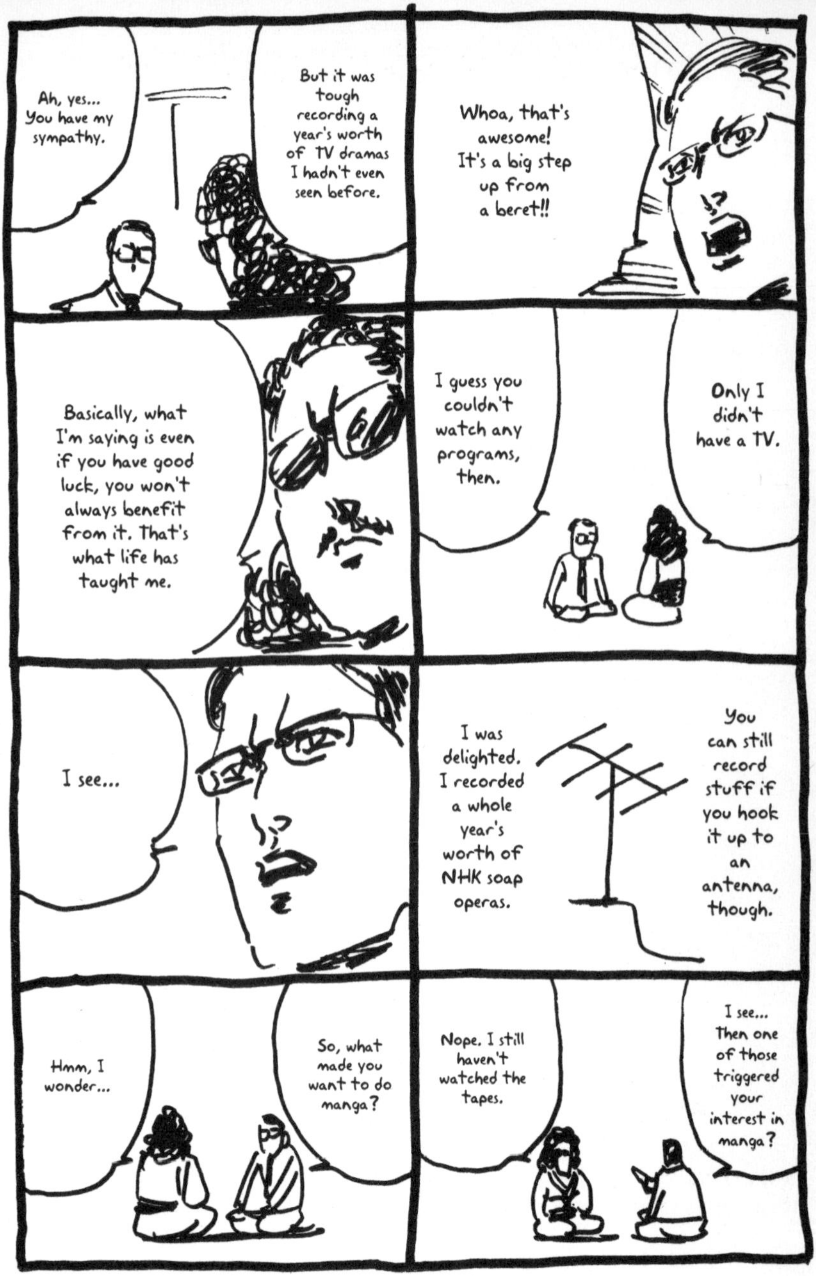
Whoa, that's awesome! It's a big step up from a beret!!
Only I didn't have a TV.
I guess you couldn't watch any programs, then.
You can still record stuff if you hook it up to an antenna, though.
I was delighted. I recorded a whole year's worth of NHK soap operas.
I see... Then one of those triggered your interest in manga?
Nope. I still haven't watched the tapes.
But it was tough recording a year's worth of TV dramas I hadn't even seen before.
Ah, yes... You have my sympathy.
Basically, what I'm saying is even if you have good luck, you won't always benefit from it. That's what life has taught me.
I see...
So, what made you want to do manga?
Hmm, I wonder...

THE END

CROMARTIE HIGH SCHOOL VOLUME ONE

© 2001 Eiji Nonaka
All rights reserved.
First published in Japan in 2001 by Kodansha Ltd., Tokyo
English translation rights for this edition arranged through Kodansha Ltd.

Translator **BRENDAN FRAYNE**
Lead Translator/Translation Supervisor **JAVIER LOPEZ**
ADV Manga Translation Staff **KAY BERTRAND & AMY FORSYTH**

Print Production/Art Studio Manager **LISA PUCKETT**
Pre-press Manager **KLYS REEDYK**
Sr. Designer/Creative Manager **JORGE ALVARADO**
Graphic Designer/Group Leader **GEORGE REYNOLDS**
Graphic Designers **NATALIA MORALES & HEATHER GARY**
Graphic Intern **MARK MEZA**

International Coordinators **TORU IWAKAMI,
ATSUSHI KANBAYASHI & KYOKO DRUMHELLER**

Publishing Editor **SUSAN ITIN**
Assistant Editor **MARGARET SCHAROLD**
Editorial Assistant **SHERIDAN JACOBS**
Editorial Intern **MIKE ESSMYER**
Research/Traffic Coordinator **MARSHA ARNOLD**

Executive VP, CFO, COO **KEVIN CORCORAN**

President, CEO & Publisher **JOHN LEDFORD**

Email: editor@adv-manga.com
www.adv-manga.com
www.advfilms.com

For sales and distribution inquiries please call 1.800.282.7202

ADV MANGA™ is a division of A.D. Vision, Inc.
10114 W. Sam Houston Parkway, Suite 200, Houston, Texas 77099

English text © 2005 published by A.D. Vision, Inc. under exclusive license.
ADV MANGA is a trademark of A.D. Vision, Inc.

ISBN: 1-4139-0257-X
First printing, March 2005
10 9 8 7 6 5 4 3 2 1
Printed in Canada

Cromartie Vol. 01

Tokyo Metropolitan
In 1943, the Tokyo Metropolitan Government was established to unite the old Tokyo-shi (Tokyo City) and Tokyo-fu (the surrounding Tokyo Prefecture). The new designation was Tokyo-to, which is still used today.

Choral Competition
Most Japanese secondary schools hold a yearly choral contest, in which each class performs a song and is judged for harmony and performance. The atmosphere is generally quite relaxed.

Yume wa Yoru Hiraku
The 1970 hit that made Keiko Utada a pop music sensation. For all the J-Pop fans out there, Keiko Utada is the mother of current star Hikaru Utada.

Commencement Ceremony
Unlike most American schools, Japanese junior high and high schools have a matriculation, or "commencement ceremony," in which incoming freshman are officially welcomed. Japanese schools also have at least some sort of ceremony at the start of each new semester.

Last Battle/Last Stand
In the first stanza of the school anthem, the Japanese text uses the term *tennozan*, which can be translated as "last/decisive battle" or "strategic point." Going back in history, *tennozan* refers to the battle of Mt. Tennozan between feudal lords Toyotomi Hideyoshi and Akechi Mitsuhide in 1582. Toyotomi won this battle, avenging the death of his lord, Oda Nobunaga, and securing his position as the shogun's successor and ruler of Japan. In a looser, modern sense, the term is used to refer to games between first and second-place teams in a league where the title is on the line.

The second stanza uses the term *sekigahara*, which has similar historical underpinnings. The Battle of the same name occurred in 1600 between *Tokugawa* Ieyasu and Ishida Mitsunari. *Tokugawa* won the battle, becoming the third great unifier of Japan and ending two years of civil strife.

Run (Errands) Towards Tomorrow!

Pg. 3 Most of the chapter titles are plays on famous movie and/or song titles. The title for Chapter 5 is not just a reference to a famous movie, but also a play on words. First, the author took the Japanese title to Butch Cassidy and the Sundance Kid (Ashita ni Mukatte Ute, lit. "Fire Away, Towards Tomorrow"), and changed the ute ("fire") to *pashire*, which means something along the lines of "run errands," or "be someone's errand boy."

Sentimental Bus

Pg. 4 The chapter 8 title refers to a Japanese rock band of the same name.

Normal de GO!

Pg. 4 The chapter title is a pun based off of the popular simulation game, **Densha de GO** (lit. "Go by train").

The Ultimate Lightness of Being

Pg. 4 The chapter 16 title in Japanese, *Sonzai no Omoikiri na Karusa*, is a spoof of the movie title, **Sonzai no Taerarenai Karusa** (aka, The Unbearable Lightness of Being).

Cromartie

Pg. 4 The Japanese title for chapter 17 was *Mirai Seiki Cromartie*, a pun of the Japanese name for the Terry Gilliam movie, **Brazil** (Mirai Seiki Brazil, lit. "Future Century Brazil").

Entrance Exams

Pg. 9 In Japan, non-standardized entrance exams are required for high schools as well as universities. Students put in intense hours of study in hopes of passing these exams and enroll in the high school/university of their choice.

Hairstyles

Pg. 18 Pompadour here refers to the 50s-style Elvis (or Fonz from Happy Days) hair cut, with a ducktail in back and the top combed flamboyantly up and over. The "kinky permanent" (or "punch perm," as the Japanese call it) is a short, tight and intensely curly hairstyle. Traditionally (and comically), both are hoodlum trademarks, and not the norm among badasses these days.

Moxa

Pg. 28 Moxa are small rolls of mugwort (an herb) which are ignited and put in either direct or indirect contact with the skin in order to increase the flow of chi throughout certain areas. Moxa are used in acupuncture/moxibustion.

Yakisoba

Pg. 31 *Yakisoba* is a popular noodle dish made by frying ramen-like flour noodles, cabbage, and occasionally other vegetables. It is served with a sweetish, brown sauce and often garnished with pickled ginger and a dollop of mayonnaise. Highly recommended!

Hirai-san the Flunker

The reason Hirai does not fit in well with his class is because in Japan grade levels are taken somewhat more seriously. Upperclassmen are referred to as *sempai* ("senior/elder/superior"), and the underclassmen, or *kouhai*, are obligated to give them a certain level of respect. The students coming up into Hirai's class are technically his kouhai, though as far as grade level is concerned, they are now his equals. As slight compensation, Kamiyama respectfully affixes the honorific -san to Hirai's name.

Teppo Practice

Teppo is a sumo practice exercise, wherein the wrestler stands in front of a wooden pole and slaps it repeatedly.

Nikko

A very popular tourist (and field trip) spot in eastern Japan. Nikko is famous for its ornate shrines and the well-known carving of the three "hear no evil, speak no evil, see no evil" monkeys. It is also the burial site of Ieyasu Tokugawa.

Iroha-zaka

Iroha-zaka is a set of twisting roads that connect urban Nikko to the outlying Lake Chuzenji. The name Iroha comes from the number of winding curves which make up the road—48, which is also the number of basic syllables in Japanese. "I, Ro, Ha" is the traditional Japanese equivalent to A, B, C.

Mountains

Cromartie High is somewhere in the Tokyo area—which is flat!

Pike

Sanma (or saury pike) are small, slender fish that are traditionally eaten in autumn. Grilled whole, they have a slightly bitter taste that balances nicely with soy sauce and sliced radish, two condiments with which it is almost always accompanied (hence Kamiyama's chagrin).

UFOs

Named after UFO photographer George Adamski, so-called "Adamski-type" UFOs are circular and feature globes or "generators" on their undersides. Cigar-shaped UFOs, by comparison are... well, cigar shaped.

Hiromi Go

Whether coincidence or no, Hiromi go is also a famous Japanese singer/media personality. He had a successful movie and TV career in the 70s and 80s, and then made a huge comeback in 1999 with a cover of Ricky Martin's "La Vida Loca."

Scores

In Japan, where grading is rather severe, a 60 does not necessarily reflect poor performance. It would more likely be somewhere between average and below average.

Tatami Mats

Tatami are rectangular straw-wrapped mats, which many Japanese homes have as flooring material in one or more rooms. They are very expensive to replace, and do wear out over time (especially if things are moved around on them a lot).

Cutting a Promo

This is pro-wrestling lingo to describe when a wrestler gets in the ring alone and proceeds to talk smack to (or about) another wrestler, or announces a challenge or surprise match. Incidentally, this was described in the text using the coined-in-Japan term "Mic Appeal."

Osamu Tezuka

Osamu Tezuka is known in Japan as the "god of manga." This legendary artist is responsible for such landmark titles as Astroboy, Blackjack, Kimba the White Lion, and many others.

NHK

Abbreviation for *"Nippon Housou Kyoukai,"* or Japan Broadcasting Association, a government-sponsored television station which features educational programs as well as soap operas and other programming. Of note among those "soap operas" are *taiga dramas*, or long-running historical (though not necessarily factual) drama series, which typically run a year or longer. Apparently, the author is a fan of these.

-san/-kun

Most people will be familiar with the Japanese tendency to affix -san to the end of last (or even first) names to increase the politeness level. -san is often equated to Ms., Mr., or Mrs. A good rule of thumb is that -san (often equated to Ms., Mr. or Mrs.) is used when addressing someone outside one's group (of friends, family, co-workers, etc.) or in some cases, superiors. Kamiyama addresses Takenouchi with –san, reflecting greater respect for this "underground kingpin."

Another term often used in this volume is -kun. Its usage varies more than -san, and is often applied when addressing a (usually, but not always, male) inferior—for example, a teacher speaking to a student. It can also be used by friends or social equals when addressing each other, as in the many instances where Kamiyama addresses Hayashida and the others.

Several more of these suffixes, or "honorifics," are employed in Japanese—some more formal, some less so, and some downright derogatory! In translation, honorifics are often dropped, as manner of speech and proper English titles can usually take their places without sacrificing social nuances. Even in Japanese, some manga make little or no use of honorifics, while others rely on them to varying degrees. The honorifics were preserved in this translation because the story takes place in the highly-stratified environment of a Japanese high school, and touches on Japanese social intricacies that others don't (For example, the predicaments of Takenouchi and Hirai the Flunker).

The hijinks of Cromartie High have gotten out of hand, but the outside world has become an even bigger threat!

Mechazawa is accidentally sold as a household appliance, and after an out-of-this-world encounter, Freddie is skipping school to become an alien companion... or a test subject.

A shift in high school royalty is now underway, and the newest bully will terrorize his classmates in a whole new way when the underlings meet their new leader in

CROMARTIE
HIGH SCHOOL VOL.2

www.adv-manga.com

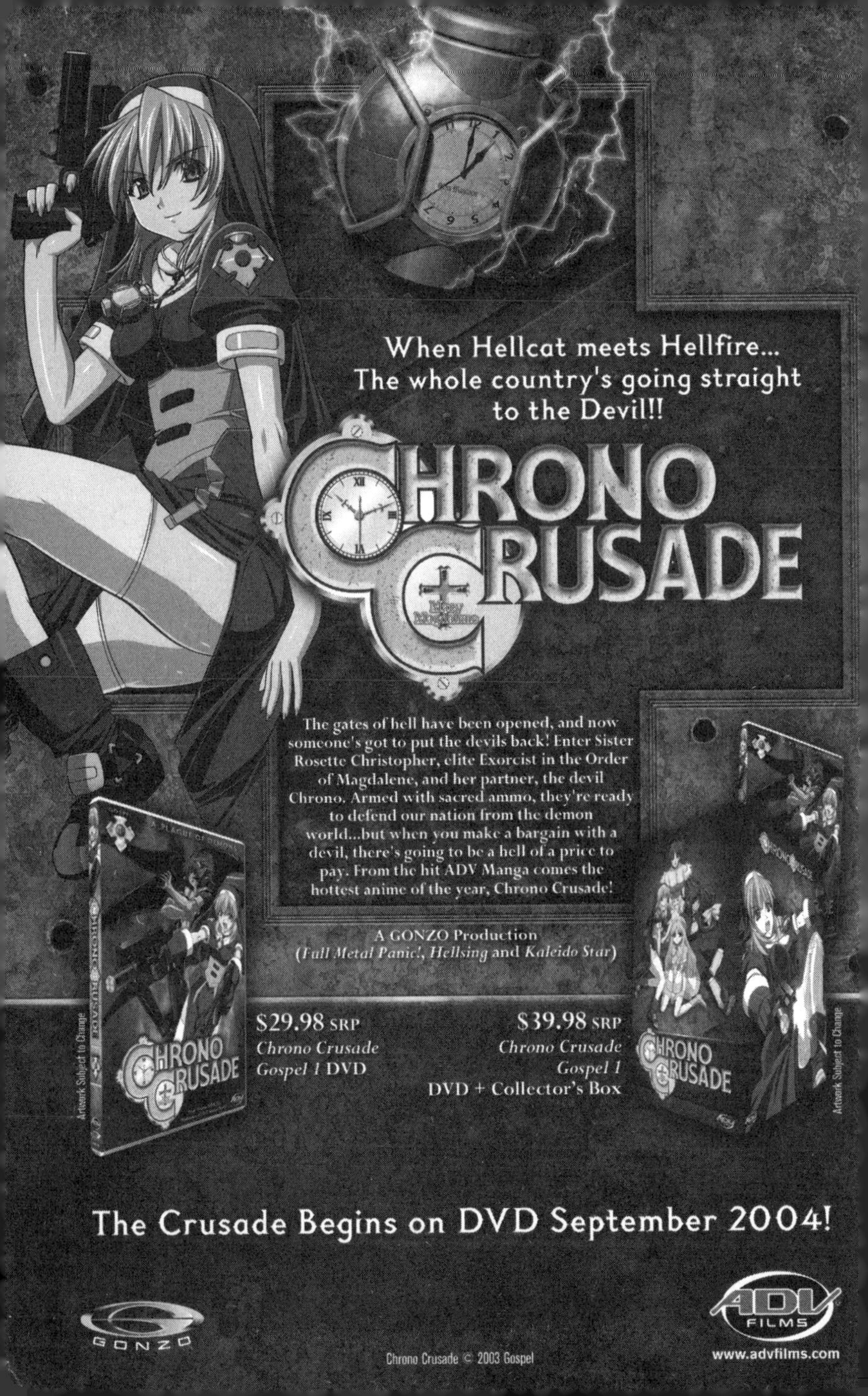

When Hellcat meets Hellfire...
The whole country's going straight to the Devil!!
CHRONO CRUSADE
The gates of hell have been opened, and now someone's got to put the devils back! Enter Sister Rosette Christopher, elite Exorcist in the Order of Magdalene, and her partner, the devil Chrono. Armed with sacred ammo, they're ready to defend our nation from the demon world...but when you make a bargain with a devil, there's going to be a hell of a price to pay. From the hit ADV Manga comes the hottest anime of the year, Chrono Crusade!
A GONZO Production
(Full Metal Panic!, Hellsing and Kaleido Star)
$29.98 SRP
Chrono Crusade
Gospel 1 DVD
$39.98 SRP
Chrono Crusade
Gospel 1
DVD + Collector's Box
Artwork Subject to Change
Artwork Subject to Change
The Crusade Begins on DVD September 2004!
GONZO
Chrono Crusade © 2003 Gospel
ADV FILMS
www.advfilms.com

S METHING MISSI G
FROM YOUR TV?

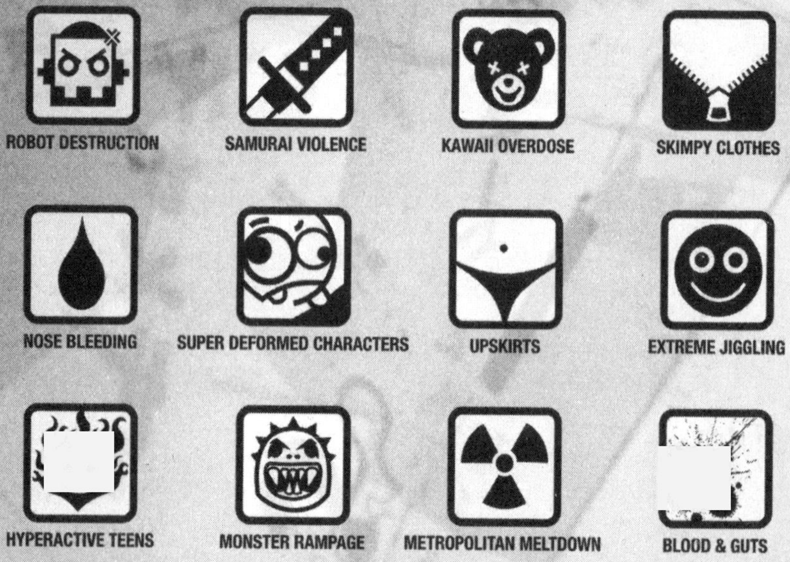
ROBOT DESTRUCTION
SAMURAI VIOLENCE
KAWAII OVERDOSE
SKIMPY CLOTHES
NOSE BLEEDING
SUPER DEFORMED CHARACTERS
UPSKIRTS
EXTREME JIGGLING
HYPERACTIVE TEENS
MONSTER RAMPAGE
METROPOLITAN MELTDOWN
BLOOD & GUTS

Tired of networks that only dabble in anime? Tired of the same old cartoons?

Demand more from your cable or satellite operator. If they don't currently offer Anime Network as part of your channel lineup, then something is missing.

Your TV deserves better.

You deserve Anime Network.

Log on and demand anime in your home 24/7:
WWW.THEANIMENETWORK.COM

ANIME NETWORK

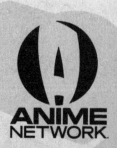

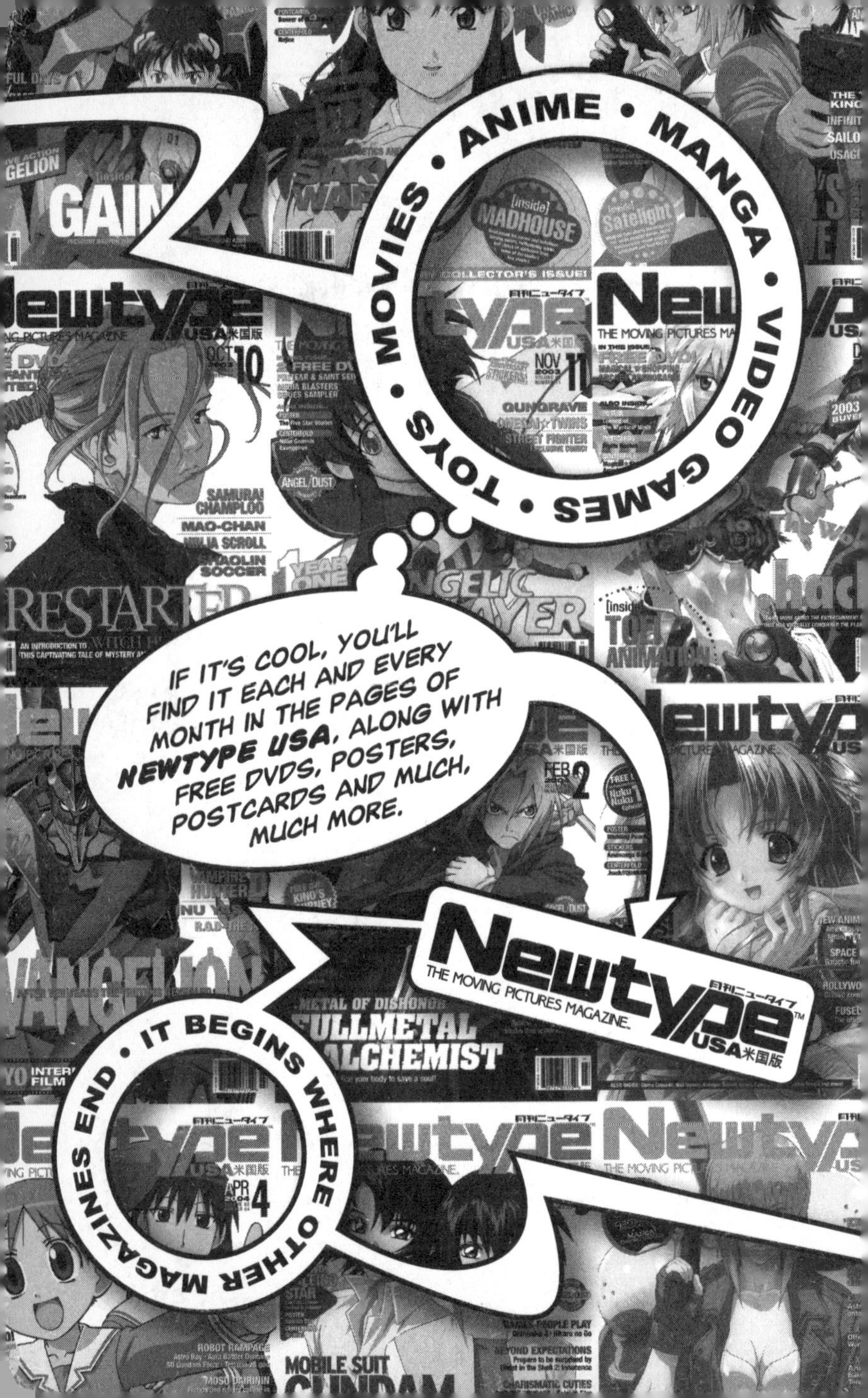
ANIME • MANGA • VIDEO GAMES • TOYS • MOVIES •
IF IT'S COOL, YOU'LL FIND IT EACH AND EVERY MONTH IN THE PAGES OF NEWTYPE USA, ALONG WITH FREE DVDS, POSTERS, POSTCARDS AND MUCH, MUCH MORE.
Newtype
THE MOVING PICTURES MAGAZINE.
USA米国版
月刊ニュータイプ
IT BEGINS WHERE OTHER MAGAZINES END •

What can you see a pig, a dog, and a...Puchu?

You head for cover!

Puchu
(from Excel Saga)

Saizo
(from Peacemaker Kurogane)

Menchi
(from Excel Saga)